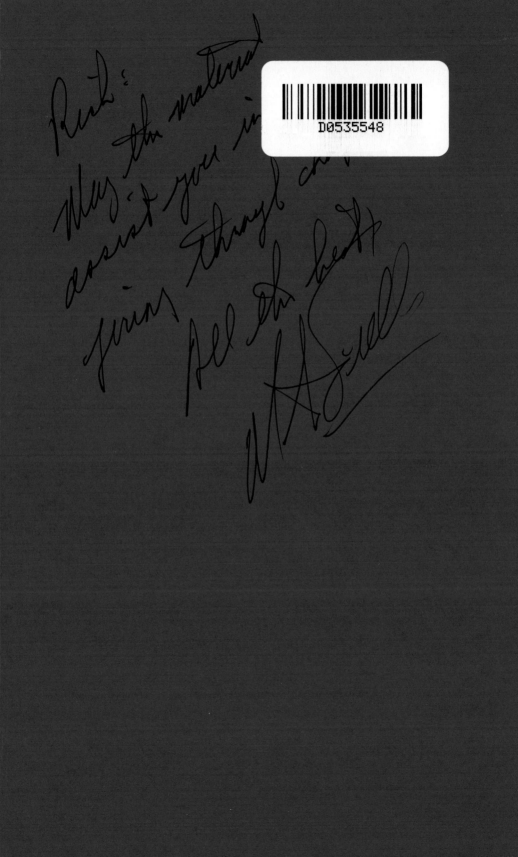

Rick:

May the material
assist you in
firing through on

All the best

Mike Fuller's seminars have won accolades from many participants. Here's what a few of them had to say:

> " I highly recommend Mike's talk on 'Footprints'. I believe it should re-focus many people's attention onto what is important to themselves."

> " Mike does a wonderful job of relating theoretical concepts with the practical world. His own... experience helps tremendously and makes him a credible source of information."

> " Very much enjoyed Mike's presentation–he ably weaved our organizational concerns into the fabric of his material. It really made learning much easier."

> " I was able to relate my personal life to my work life in all of Mike's sessions. Many of the ideas presented are now recorded for action."

Mark Kingsbury, President of Canadian Mountain Holidays, says:

> " Mike Fuller helped us through a critical strategic stage in our corporate development. He combines an academic perspective with real life understanding that is refreshing and valuable when leading managers through any planning process... In the world of personal consultants, Mike comes out as one of the highest value adders around."

James Graham, Deputy Chief of the Calgary Police Service, says:

> " It is obvious when listening to Mike that he not only understands the theory of total quality service but that he has a very extensive repertoire of work-related examples... To step into the police culture and immediately relate to career police officers demonstrates the depth of Mike's ability to communicate his subject matter."

Inge Frethiem, President, Canadian Marine Drilling (CANMAR), says:

" Mike played a key role in several efforts to improve the way we apply the process of management and leadership to our business–his professional approach, knowledge and good sense of humor, made a strong impression on all of us. "

Alain Gaumier, President and CEO, Canadian Surety - Canada West, says:

" Mike Fuller's insight and sensitivity towards the requirements of leadership and his future vision and understanding of organizations and management structures been have invaluable to our company. "

If you are interested in having Mike do seminars for you, he can be reached through:

- Pauline Price of CANSPEAK (Vancouver),
  at 1-800-665-7376, (604) 986-6887,
  fax (604) 986-6803

- Sheree McGarrity of CANSPEAK (Peterborough),
  at 1-800-561-3591, (705) 741-2992,
  fax (705) 743-4325

- Susan McMaster (Calgary), at (403) 244-4067

In the United States Mike can be booked through:

- Tony Calao at MasterMedia Limited (New Jersey),
  at 1(800) 453-2887, (908) 359-1612,
  fax (908) 359-1647

Above
The Bottom Line

**Building Business Success
through Individual Growth**

J. MICHAEL FULLER
with ALAN HOBSON

Canadian Cataloguing in Publication Data

Fuller, J. Michael Fuller, 1942-

    Above the bottom line: building business success
    through individual growth

ISBN   0-7715-9360-0

1. Success in business. 2. Organizational effectiveness.
3. Success. I. Hobson, Alan, 1959- . II. Title.

HF5386.F85 1993   650.1   C93-094440-2

Macmillan Canada wishes to thank the Canada Council and the Ontario Ministry of Culture and Communications for supporting its publishing program.

Edited by Leslie Johnson, Susan McMaster and Erika Krolman

Book design and graphics by Debi Whistlecraft

Macmillan Canada
A Division of Canada Publishing Corporation
Toronto, Canada

1 2 3 4 5 TG 97 96 95 94 93

Printed in Canada

DEDICATION

This book is dedicated to those closest to me. Gisela, my wife, taught me patience and wisdom. She has loved me and put up with me for many years. She is without question my best friend.

My children have taught me forgiveness. I've made a lot of mistakes with them over the years and they have always forgiven me.

My father taught me humor. He encouraged me not to take life too seriously, and above all to treat people with respect and generosity.

My late mother put me in touch with myself. She gave me the sensitivity to see the emotional side of my life and appreciate its value.

If you read something that inspires you, it probably came from one of them.

THE WHO, WHAT, WHEN, WHY AND HOW OF THIS BOOK

Who should read this book?

If you're a life-long learner, interested in self-improvement, or want to see how you might improve organizations to which you belong, you should read this book. Anyone who is going through changes–within or outside their control–should also read it. It may help them to regain some control.

What do you need to benefit from this book?

You need two things to understand what is in this book. The two things are:

1. A firm belief in yourself–that you **can** make a difference.

2. A belief in others–so they can learn to believe in themselves.

If you have these two beliefs, you will come to understand what Peter Block, author of *The Empowered Manager*, wrote:

> *Within each of us is the ability to create an organization of our own choosing.*

When should you read this book?

This book is an easy read, but to apply the principles outlined in it, you will have to think a lot–sometimes deeply. Thus, **don't** read this book when you're in a rush.

You'll need to have time to think about the concepts in this book, and how to apply them. If you never have time for yourself, it's time to start. If you don't take the time to actually apply the concepts, you won't get the maximum benefit from this book. If you invest the time, your return will be well worth it.

Why should you read this book?

This book may help you discover a greater understanding of yourself and the organizations where you work and live. It should provide you with the tools to stay on track personally and professionally.

Why did I write this book?

I wrote this book because I carried experience and information inside me that I wanted to share. A large portion of it was all of the things I had learned in some 25 years of business in all sizes of organizations, including universities.

I have had the privilege of working with people as salesman, team builder, teacher, seminar leader, program developer and currently as a consultant with middle and senior managers. The reward has been seeing the positive effect my efforts have had on others.

I hope this book leaves you with a deeper understanding of who you are, encourages you to understand the value you give to yourself and to your community, and enhances the legacy you leave behind.

This book is from the heart. I hope you take it to heart. May it inspire you, encourage you, and uplift you.

Where did all the ideas come from?

This book is filled with my ideas and experiences. But many others have influenced my life. Authors like Peter Block (*The Empowered Manager*); Max DePree (*Leadership Is an Art*); Robert Fulghum (*All I Really Need to Know I Learned in Kindergarten*); and James Allen (*As a Man Thinketh*) have been particularly influential. So have faculty members at the University of Calgary in Alberta, Canada. Some worked with me in launching the first executive development program at the university. Getting eight Ph.D's to become team players is considered a miracle in some quarters. But we did it. They proved to me that solitary eagles not only can fly, they can also flock. And, I believe, we enhanced our faculty and the university in the process.

I have had the pleasure of working with many managers/ leaders and teachers over the years. The good ones taught me how personal discipline and risk-taking could enhance their lives and their organizations–even when they were not totally sure of themselves or where they were headed. Business mavericks like Garry Mihaichuk of Amoco, CEOs like Arvid Petersen of Blackwoods Beverages (Pepsi-Cola) of Calgary (now of Australia), Dr. Walter Wright Jr., Regent College in Vancouver, B.C., and my father, John C. J. Fuller, who made a lot of money for a lot of people: these people have had the biggest influence in developing "The Footprint" model I introduce with Alan Hobson in this book.

Several leading companies that I have been involved with have also substantially affected me. They include IBM Canada, Hewlett-Packard and Xerox International. Those I studied–Walmart, General Electric, Levi Strauss and Lincoln Electric have also had a great impact.

I have had the pleasure of working as a group chairman with dozens of CEOs from mid-sized firms through a San Diego, California-based management training organization called The Executive Committee (TEC), which has thousands of members worldwide. In particular, I would like to thank consultant, seminar leader and fellow TEC chairman, John Konstanturos, of Del Mar, California. He is the primary influence behind the Purpose Footprint of this book. John's influence enriched the Organizational Purpose Step and helped me understand the need to introduce the Individual Footprint.

TABLE OF CONTENTS

INTRODUCTION

The not-to-be-skipped part of this book

FOOTPRINT ONE
The Power of Purpose

Part I : Personal Purpose

Why are we all here anyway?

Part II : Organizational Purpose

What do we offer to the world around us other than the manufacture and delivery of products and services?

FOOTPRINT TWO
The Value of Vision

Part I : Personal Vision

What do I want to "look like" when I "grow up"?

Part II: Organizational Vision

What does my organization want to become?

FOOTPRINT THREE
The Force of Focus

Part I : Personal Focus

What is my personal beacon in life?

Part II : Organizational Focus

What significant activities should my people be energized towards?

FOOTPRINT FOUR
The Soft (Hard-to-Do) Stuff

Part I : Individual

What activities will help me to become who I say I want to be?

What brings groups of people together to accomplish common goals?

FOOTPRINT FIVE
Brilliancies in Behavior

Part I : Individual

What are the behaviors necessary to actualize my purpose, vision and focus?

FOOTPRINT SIX
The Bottom Line

264

264

Part II : Organizational

How do we know people are doing what we expect of them?

EPILOGUE

AFTERWORD

NOTES

In any discussion of how to improve bottom-line results in an organization, we must first study how to improve ourselves as individuals. I believe that individual and organizational greatness are inseparable.

If you doubt this, ask yourself if you know an organization that is struggling. Then ask yourself if you know an organization that is succeeding. What is the common element to both situations? If you answer "a person," then we begin to understand each other.

INTRODUCTION

This is not an introduction. Introductions
are optional reading. This is essential.

*Managing only for profits is like playing tennis
with your eye on the scoreboard and not on
the ball.*

DONALD E. PETERSEN
Former chairman
Ford Motor Company

*We didn't all come over on the same ship,
but we're all in the same boat.*

BERNARD BARUCH
American financier,
statesman

Setting the stage

It's 2:00 a.m. in the mid-Atlantic, 1944. As you sleep soundly in your bunk, a submarine slips stealthily into range. With a single move of an index finger, the captain delivers the signal.

Seconds later, your whole world turns upside down. With a deafening blast, a torpedo rips through the hull. Thousands of gallons of frigid ocean pour in below decks.

You jackknife up in bed. Your head slams full force into the bunk above. For a moment, you are totally disoriented. As blood begins to trickle down your face, chaos shoots through the ship. Alarm bells blast. Bunks explode in a frantic flurry of sailors and blankets.

You grab your flashlight. Men are screaming. You try to shake sense into yourself. It's useless.

In a near-paralysed panic, you flail your way from below. Every step is a blur.

Suddenly, the ship lurches sideways. You stumble. Then, the movement stops momentarily. Seeing your chance, you scramble up the final steps on deck. There, you discover all the life rafts are taken. You struggle into a life jacket and dive into the icy water.

Instantly, your chest muscles contract from the cold. For a terrifying moment, you can't breathe. It's like someone knocked the wind out of you. You surface and gasp for air. Finally, your chest muscles begin to relax. You start swimming –you give it everything you have. You know that if you don't get as far away from the ship as possible, you could be sucked into the depths with it.

2

There's a terrible screech. Steel twists, curls and collapses. A blast of cold air issues from the depths as the wreck exhales for the last time. A geyser of ice-cold water shoots skyward. It hits you with the force of a fire hose.

You wait for the undertow...nothing. There's silence...nothing but silence.

You look around you. In an instant, you realize you are totally alone–alone in the Atlantic–your only means of physical support disappearing forever into a boiling vortex of water...

▲　　▲　　▲　　▲

When merchant vessels were sunk during World War II, per 1,000 men in each age group, more younger men died than older ones. Naval officials were stumped. The younger sailors were supposed to be more physically fit, better able to adapt, quicker to react.

Experts could only hypothesize–when their ship went down, did the young mariners lose their symbol of security, their touchstone to life? Like children clinging to their mother, when the mother left, did life leave too?

One of the world's most well-known achievement organizations, Outward Bound, was founded during this time. Its aim was straightforward, but not simple: turn the tide of youthful death in the Atlantic. In response to the challenge, the organization's founders deliberately put young men into extreme outdoor adventure situations in all types of terrain–from the mountains, to the seas, deserts and jungles. Their hope was to show young sailors how to stretch beyond the security of their perceived limits into the unknown arena of their actual potential. In short, the program trained them to survive insecurity.

Our metaphorical ships

In a very real way, we are all afloat on an ocean of insecurity. We are unsure of the future, unsure whether we will have a job tomorrow, even unsure of a secure family. If our ship went down today, would we survive?

> *Security is mostly a superstition. It does not exist in nature, nor do the children of men as a whole experience it. Life is either a daring adventure or nothing.*
>
> HELEN KELLER
> American essayist
> and lecturer

Security in all its forms–professional, financial, health, family, whatever–is vanishing from the Western world. Declining world economies, the high divorce rate, the increasing incidence of heart disease and cancer and eroding natural resources have taken a catastrophic toll on the citizens of the West–both individually and organizationally. Hundreds of thousands have been laid off. Many find themselves struggling through job loss, marriage breakup, life-threatening disease and family violence. Some have lost hope.

This book offers some respite from it all. First, it suggests new definitions of "success"–ones that are more achievable, realistic and enduring. Second, it presents a step-by-step procedure for improving your quality of life–and reducing human distress.

Floating on the sea of life

Every one of us is on a voyage through life. To some extent, we all cling to "ships" of one sort or another. Some of us cling to family and friends, others to organizations and institutions, others to ourselves. Some of us are on ships afloat in calm seas, others in turbulent waters. All of us can sink. Regardless of our situation, however, if we are to survive and thrive in the twenty-first century, we need to become more self-sufficient. In short, we must learn how to survive without our ships–alone, if necessary.

> *And this is the simple truth: that to live is to feel oneself lost. He who accepts it has already begun to find himself, to be on firm ground...Instinctively, as do the shipwrecked, he will look around for something to which to cling; and that tragic, ruthless glance, absolutely sincere because it is a question of his salvation, will cause him to bring order into the chaos of his life. These are the only genuine ideas of the shipwrecked. All the rest is rhetoric, posturing, farce.* [1]

> SOREN KIERKEGAARD
> Danish philosopher

Who should read this book?

This book is written for those who want to improve themselves, their lives or the organizations to which they belong. It is designed to provide a life support system that goes beyond life's conventional "ships"–job, family, health or church. Although these ships are significant in our lives, we are more significant. I use the word "organization" often in this book. I do so loosely. An organization can be anything from a couple to a family; a baseball team to a battalion. In the corporate sense, it implies a company. It's any ship.

This book is not written just for managers of companies, but indeed for managers of everything from relationships to families, from bowling leagues to bridge nights. It is written for everyone from teenagers to CEOs, from entrepreneurs to homemakers–anyone who can be cast into the depths, or rise up in triumph at a moment's notice.

If you are:

- an individual
- a member of a couple or partnership (a two-member organization)
- a member of a family (a multi-member organization)
- a member of a business, government, charity or non-profit group (a multi-level organization)

... this book is for you.

All hands on deck

We are all captains of our own ships and we sail (and sometimes founder) along as members of organizations. Some of us manage people, others money, others products, still others processes. All of us manage, and sometimes mismanage, ourselves.

If you want to improve your "sailing" skills, this book is for you. It is both a personal and organizational achievement book. If you disregard it because you think it's meant for executives and can only be used at the office, you may miss 90 per cent of its worth.

The strength of this book lies in your hands right now– in how you read it, how you use it and, most importantly, how you actually apply it to **your** life today and tomorrow. You can choose to survive and thrive, sink or swim.

The big and little picture

The achievement and self-improvement process you are about to undertake can be applied to any aspect of your life–from choosing a career to planting a garden or constructing a home. You can use it to raise your family or raise your self-esteem, to run a business or run a race.

As you read this book, try to bring to mind all the challenges–large and small–you are currently facing. Then, using the steps outlined here, try to apply this system for success to your personal, professional or family life.

I have used the system I outline in this book with a great deal of effectiveness in many areas of my life–from my own work in major organizations to my subsequent speaking and management consulting business and family life. It's astounding what you can do with it if you just use your imagination. To realize the system's universality, you have to use your creativity.

Choices

Talent, it's been said, is nothing without opportunity. This book is an opportunity for you. You can choose to capitalize (literally or figuratively) on it, or you can just let it gather dust on your bookshelf. The choice is yours.

What this book is all about

This book has four goals:

1 to show individuals and organizations how to focus on what produces results, rather than on the results themselves

2 to introduce new measures of success which can produce better results

3 to encourage you to follow the steps here to help you achieve self-fulfilment and

4 to show the significant relationship between individual

A confession

This isn't really a book about the bottom line. It's about what needs to happen above the bottom line to produce that bottom line. Too many individuals and organizations focus on the end results without truly understanding how those results are actually achieved. Like the score in any game, what counts most is what happens on the field of play. Why? Because what happens on the field of play produces the score.

This, then, isn't a book about how to improve profits–however you define that word. It's about how to improve your personal and professional bottom lines. Bottom lines mean more than money. They include personal contentment, self-confidence, self-esteem and self-actualization. And, as any leader will tell you–parent, manager, CEO or minister–when you improve individuals, you improve individual and organizational bottom lines.

From individual to organizational greatness

Every day individuals within organizations make important decisions. Yet many do not recognize the critical relationship between the individuals within their organization and the organization as a whole. It's only after we know where we are going as individuals that we can make a lasting contribution to any type of organization.

Why, you may ask, would anyone write a leadership book in this way?

In any discussion of how to improve bottom line results in an organization, we must first study how to improve ourselves as individuals. I believe that individual and organizational greatness are inseparable.

If you doubt this, ask yourself if you know an organization that is struggling. Then ask yourself if you know an organization that is succeeding. What is the element common to both situations? If you answer "a person," then we begin to understand each other. In a couple, that person can be one or both partners. In a corporation, it can be an extraordinary employee or employees.

> *Rather dramatic changes in the performance of divisions occurred when the only thing that had changed in the division was the leader.* [2]
>
> PHILIP SMITH
> Chairman, General Foods

No one can effectively lead others without first knowing, and therefore leading, themselves. We have to start at the personal level in this book. If we start at the organizational level, we put the cart before the horse. The horse is you. The cart is the organization to which you belong. Thus, you come first. Your organization comes second. That may surprise some people. They mistakenly believe that to succeed as an organization, the individual members must give it everything they have.

This does not mean we should not work hard. It does mean we should know when to work and, just as importantly, when to relax. No true success can come without it.

From sea to land –
The evolution of excellence

Although we are afloat on a sea of insecurity and the unknown, let's bring this whole achievement, self-help issue back to shore.

9

Successful individuals and organizations, as *In Search of Excellence* and *The 7 Habits of Highly Effective People* determined, possess certain characteristics. I like to call these characteristics **the Footprints** they leave behind. This book is really about the footprints you and your organizations leave behind. At sea, the trail vanishes quickly in our wake. On earth, however, our legacy can last longer–if we live life right.

Tracing the track record of success

As you know, footprints come in all sizes and shapes. But the footprints of successful individuals and organizations have certain characteristics in common. In fact, if you follow their footprints over time, a common path emerges. It is the track record of excellence.

Sometimes the track record is short. For some successful individuals and organizations, it is enduring.

> *Perseverance is not a long race; it is many short races one after another.*
>
> WALTER ELLIOTT

The length of the track record is not the most important thing to look at in evaluating the lasting effect of an individual or organization. The positive effect individuals have on themselves and on others can be the most important factor in determining success.

Getting on track

I am confident that if you follow the steps outlined in this book, you and your organization will leave behind footprints that have a lasting impression. It will be a path others will want to follow.

Fuller's Footprints –
The lasting impression of this book

Let's look at the steps we're about to take.This book is built around six chapters, or steps. These form **the Footprints** of the manuscript:

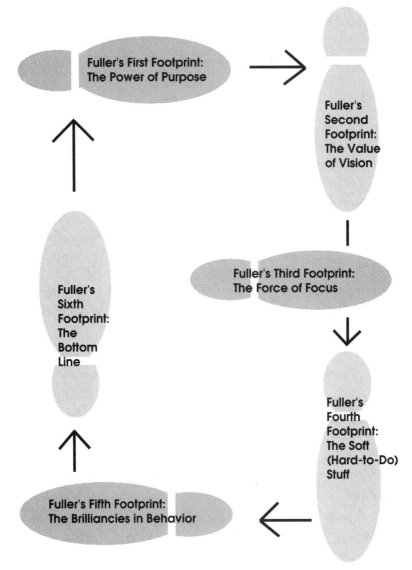

How to read this book

The Footprints are designed to take you step-by-step through the process of individual and organizational achievement. Each Footprint has two parts: **Part I, Individual** (the heel, if you like) and **Part II, Organizational** (the toe).

THE TOTAL FOOTPRINT

If you just want to read this book for your own benefit, read only the individual parts of each Footprint. If you're in it for both individual and organizational benefit, read both parts of each Footprint.

This book is both a step-by-step guide and a workbook. Each Footprint includes questions and exercises. They are designed to show you how to put the ideas in each Footprint into practice.

The result should be something far different from many other personal or organizational achievement books. This book doesn't just talk about theories or principles. It shows you how to actually apply them to your personal and organizational lives.

The Footprints explained

Fuller's First Footprint: The Power of Purpose

The First Footprint introduces you to the benefits of knowing why you and/or your organization are on this earth. That may sound intimidating, but actually, it isn't. After a general discussion of The Power of Purpose, numerous anecdotes and research citations illustrate how people have put this knowledge into practice. This is followed by descriptions and exercises that will enable you to actually write down your individual and organizational purposes.

12

Fuller's Second Footprint: The Value of Vision

Once we've established **why** we want to go somewhere (our Purpose), we have to choose **who** we want to be when we reach the objective (our Vision).

The Value of Vision asks you to imagine what you wish to be known for in the future. Again, following a general discussion of The Value of Vision, there are exercises designed to help create this vision individually and organizationally.

Fuller's Third Footprint: The Force of Focus

Once we've established **why** we want to go somewhere (our Purpose), **who** we want to be when we get there (our Vision), we next have to determine **where** to concentrate our energies (our Focus).

In this Footprint, you will determine how to use focus to achieve your purpose and vision individually and organizationally. It also includes a brief discussion followed by hands-on exercises.

Fuller's Fourth Footprint: The Soft (Hard to Do) Stuff

The Soft Stuff is the heart of this book. After Footprints 1, 2 and 3, you will know **why** you wish to achieve something (Purpose), **who** you want to be when you reach the objective (Vision) and **where** to concentrate your energies (Focus), the next step is to determine **what** you need to get there (the Soft Stuff). What physical and psychological tools will you require en route?

Since the Soft Stuff is the area in which most individuals and organizations fail, the Fourth Footprint is the longest and most detailed of those in the book. This Footprint will discuss the relative worth of several key forms of individual and

13

Fuller's Fifth Footprint: The Brilliancies in Behavior

All the changes we decide to make–whether they are personal or organizational–are no good if they are not acted upon. Intent is useless without action.

For any process to be effective, it must produce the desired behavior, not just at the leadership level, but at all levels. So, the Fifth Footprint will deal with the visible behaviors we need to achieve our purpose, vision and focus.

Fuller's Sixth Footprint: The Bottom Line

How we measure the results of our journey is not nearly as important as the journey itself. Therefore, this Footprint will not focus on income, status, possessions, place of residence, budgets, profits or net revenue. Instead, it will focus on other measures of achievement, among them balance, honesty, integrity, kindness and courage.

Use it or lose it

If you don't actually practise the procedures in this book, you may lose their potential benefit. Or, to make my point more direct: **Use it or lose it!**

Your first step to success

Most of us, whether we like it or not, are ordinary. I didn't say average. I said ordinary. The exciting thing is that **there is extraordinary even in the ordinary.**

Greatness knows no social or economic class; it has no geographical or linguistic boundaries, and it can flourish almost anywhere. It is, therefore, within our grasp.

14

My goal in writing this book is to bring out that element of the extraordinary in all of us. I intend to show you how to bridge the gap between what might be and what could be in your life at home, at work and at play.

To quote a famous Chinese proverb: **"The journey of a thousand miles begins with a single step."** If you have the spirit of adventure, if you're a risk-taker, a frame-breaker and a pioneer, it's time to leave the swaying seas, come ashore and set off into the woods. Ahead of you lies a set of footprints waiting to be made. The journey begins.

FOOTPRINT ONE

The Power of Purpose

All glory comes from daring to begin.

WILLIAM SHAKESPEARE

It's better to be a lion for a day than a sheep all your life.

SISTER ELIZABETH KENNY
Australian nurse

The black door

In the latter part of the Dark Ages, there was a king who regularly sentenced the country's offenders. Whenever he imposed the death sentence, he would offer the offender an option of certain death by hanging or the opportunity to walk through a black door located nearby. The catch was that if they chose the black door, they had to accept whatever consequences lay beyond. No one took him up on his offer.

One day, a trusted servant went to the king.

"Your majesty," he said, "what lies beyond the black door?"

"Freedom," replied the king.

"Then why," said the servant, "don't those sentenced to certain death choose it?"

The king paused. He examined the servant closely. Should he tell him? he asked himself. Would such a young man be capable of understanding the answer? Finally, the king rose. Standing before his throne, he proclaimed:

"Because, my curious friend, most people would prefer to accept even certain death rather than risk the unknown."

This book is about black doors. I want to encourage you to take some risks–to take some steps you wouldn't normally take. I want you to go through some black doors.

I'm going to ask you several questions in this footprint. Indeed, I'll keep asking you questions throughout this book. Some of these questions will take you into the unknown. You may find them unsettling. You may not immediately know the answers to them. Regardless of your answers, if you have the courage to answer the questions, you may find new freedom in these pages.

17

Where we're going

This chapter is divided into two parts:

Part I: Personal Purpose

a. a discussion of the importance of personal purpose

b. questions that will enable you to develop your own personal purpose statement

Part II: Organizational Purpose

a. a discussion of the importance of organizational purpose

b. questions that will enable you to develop a purpose statement for the organization(s) to which you belong

Part I: Personal Purpose

We have a hopeful future only if we stop asking what we can produce and begin to ask what we want to create. Our dignity lies not in exhausting ourselves in work but in discovering our vocation. [1]

SAM KEEN
Author, psychologist

For a minute, I'd like you to imagine you're standing outside a forest. There is a trail leading into it, but you're not sure if you wish to go down it. The challenges ahead of you are unknown. You cannot see into the woods and you cannot see through to the other side.

Naturally, you hesitate. In an attempt to gain control over the situation, you begin to ask yourself some questions: Why do I want to go into the woods? What do I hope to gain there and what information do I need before I can comfortably take the trail? If there is no trail, how do I, or should I, make my own trail?

18

The forest of life

In many ways, life is like a forest. It can be full of enjoyment and adventure. Or, it can be a struggle just to survive. As none of us have been down our trail before, we must improvise as we go along.

In our travels through the forest of life, we meet many obstacles. In our personal lives, these obstacles can include a lack of acceptance by our peers; academic and educational challenges; relationship, marriage or family problems; financial threats; layoffs; lawsuits; or the decline of physical and mental health associated with aging.

Walking through the forest can be dangerous, but it can also be exciting. If we know our purpose in being there, our ability to face and overcome these and other obstacles will markedly improve.

There's just one problem–we're already in the woods. Sooner or later, our resolve will be tested, if it hasn't happened already. If we don't know why we're there, chances are we'll either fail to rise to the challenge or we'll retreat. Those in life who know their real purpose stand the greatest chance of succeeding.

> *To be a whole man; to attain serenity through the creation of a family life of uncommon richness; through leadership of a business which brings happiness to its workers, serves well its customers and brings prosperity to its owners; by aiding a society threatened by fratricidal division to gain unity.* 2
>
> Found in the wallet of JOSEPH C. WILSON, JR. former CEO of Xerox, upon his death

The number of people who know their personal purpose is very small. But without a knowledge of why we are here, we cannot choose proper goals to fulfil our purpose. Without goals, we drift through life.

Only three per cent of the population engages in personal goalsetting. Coincidentally, only three per cent of the population ever becomes independently wealthy.

THE WORLD MASTER
TIME MANAGEMENT SYSTEM

Hiking to the top

When I was a kid, I had to pack my bag for those overnight hiking trips into the woods at summer camp. To make the job easier, the camp counsellors laid out all the group gear in front of each hiking troop. Then, each hiker had to choose what they wanted to carry for the ten-mile hike to the campsite.

Toilet paper was always one of the first items to disappear. Lack of experience led to a heavy pack of canned goods, bulky tents and unwieldy axes, shovels and canvas tarps. Inevitably, the smallest, youngest and newest campers carried the heavy gear.

This is precisely what happened to me my first year at camp. I struggled up the hills, pouring with sweat in the hot summer sun while the older, experienced veterans languished happily and smugly at the rear. The purpose of the hike, as the veterans knew, was to reach the campsite with as little effort as possible. Unfortunately, it took me a year to learn that. Had I assessed the purpose of the exercise in the first place, I could have saved myself unnecessary work.

The power of purpose

Without purpose, we seem to stagger under self-inflicted loads, while those wiser carry the lighter packs. As was the case at camp, **why** we set out to reach a goal is important.

You are not here merely to make a living. You are here in order to enable the world to live more amply, with greater vision, with a finer spirit of hope and achievement. You are to enrich the world, and you impoverish yourself if you forget the errand.

WOODROW WILSON
28th president
of the United States

Goals are important to all of us–whether we're teenagers, adults, parents, managers, employees or CEOs. We don't like to do things unless there's a good reason for it. The better the reason, the more willing we are to pursue the goal.

What the leaders of many organizations, including families, often forget is that **to attain an organizational goal, the individual members of that organization must believe it is worthwhile.** To simply announce an organizational move and expect individuals to fall swiftly into line is folly. This might seem like common sense to you, but you'd be surprised how few leaders use individual and organizational goal alignment to achieve organizational excellence. Somehow, somewhere, the individual gets lost.

In truth, there is always a give-and-take, ebb-and-flow interchange between individual and organizational purpose. Sometimes, individual purposes take precedence over organizational ones. At other times, the opposite is true.

A case in point is marriage. Marriage (organizational) difficulties often occur when one of the partners (individual) behaves without regard for the other partner or the family relationship. Families are at risk when individual careers, hobbies or personal purposes continually take precedence over the family. There are times when the family does not take precedence, but these should be the exception rather than the rule. Selfishness can destroy partnerships.

21

One of the purposes of a marriage, as I see it, is mutual support. Each partner benefits from the presence of the other. Ideally, both *need* each other.

Organizational purpose overriding individual purpose

In the 1940s a survey listed the top seven discipline problems in public schools: talking, chewing gum, making noise, running in the halls, getting out of turn in line, wearing improper clothes, not putting paper in wastebaskets. A 1980s survey lists these top seven: drug abuse, alcohol abuse, pregnancy, suicide, rape, robbery, assault. (Arson, gang warfare, and venereal disease are also-rans.)

GEORGE F. WILL
American news
commentator and author

Children and parents also need each other. Recent research on children in the United States, however, raises a serious question about the purpose of parents. According to a recent study:

- Of the 65 million Americans under 18, 22 per cent (14.3 million) live in single-parent homes

- Almost 3 per cent (1.95 million) live with no parent at all

- The parents of nearly 2,750 children separate or divorce each day

- Every day more than three children die of injuries inflicted by abusive parents

- Some 1.3 million latchkey kids aged 5 to 14 are left to fend for themselves for much of the day

- Over 1,400 teenage girls a day–two-thirds of them unmarried–become parents [3]

I don't mean to oversimplify what is a tremendously complex problem, but I do wish to present at least part of the solution: I believe most of the problems we're facing in the West stem from a lack of individual purpose and the negative effect of this on our society–a huge, multi-dimensional organization. Basically, what's being passed along to the next generation is confused, misdirected and misaligned. Too many people–many of them parents–are floating around trying desperately to find their direction.

Step One–
Developing a personal purpose statement

> *He who knows others is clever; he who knows himself is enlightened.*
>
> LAO-TZU (6th century B.C.)
> Chinese philosopher and
> founder of Taoism

Welcome to the first step on your trail to personal and/or organizational greatness. The objective of this step is to develop a statement that clearly expresses your **purpose** in life. It should be no more than 15 words long.

If the thought of developing your own purpose statement scares you, have faith. Reach for a pen and paper and step up to your first black door.

Knock, knock. Who's there?

I'm going to ask you a series of questions. They are intended more to start your creative wheels turning than anything else. You don't have to answer them. You just have to consider them.

Next, I'll ask you to make a list of words that indicate what you see as important in your life.

Finally, you'll be asked to write a statement using two or three of the words from your list.

Step One

Read and try to answer the questions below. If one stumps you because you don't understand it, don't worry about it. Go to the next one. The questions are intended to be considered as a whole, not individually.

- Why are you on Earth?

- What brings you joy?

- What do you expect out of life, work, leisure?

- What is the source of your power?

- What energizes you?

- As you look at your life, what has been a common thread that has provided you with what you have now?

- What is the primary principle for which you stand?

- What brings you peace?

- What are your gifts or talents?

- What does life mean to you?

I remember the first time I considered these questions. If you're anything like me, you are now either sweating heavily or suffering from irregular heart rhythm. Whatever your reaction, a few words and ideas should now be floating around in your head.

Step Two

■ Write down a few words that indicate what's important to you. They should be many of the same ones you are already thinking of, plus others that might describe your feelings. Don't "check" what you write–just let your thoughts flow. Fill as many of the following blanks as possible. Take no more than two minutes. Go for it now...

My words to live by

_____ _____

_____ _____

_____ _____

_____ _____

_____ _____

_____ _____

_____ _____

When you're done...

■ Take a closer look at the words you have written. Circle three you feel are most important to you. (Don't throw away the others on the list! We'll be using them later in this book.)

The three words that best describe my personal purpose are

_____

_____

_____

■ **Write a short sentence using these words. For brevity, try to stick close to 15 words. It might help to start your sentence with a word ending in "ing." Here are three examples:**

● Living my life as a role model for my friends and family.

● Leaving a legacy of improved people and organizations.

● Empowering people to achieve results through changing their processes, behaviors and attitudes.

Write your purpose here:

My personal purpose statement

_____

_____

_____

_____

The statement you have written may evolve over time, or it may not. To really work for you, it needs to become ingrained in your psyche–a type of higher personal purpose for living. You might want to put it in a prominent place where you live or work so you can periodically remind yourself of what you stand for. **Remember, only by being in touch with ourselves can we hope to positively touch and lead others.**

> *Nobody grows old by living a number of years. People grow old by deserting their ideals. Years wrinkle the skin; but to give up enthusiasm wrinkles the soul. Worry, doubt, self-distrust, fear and despair–these are the long years that bow the heart and turn the greening spirit to dust.*
>
> ANONYMOUS

26

Part II: Organizational Purpose

Western philosophy says that work exists to provide goods and services...Eastern philosophy says that work exists to enhance the human spirit. [4]

PETER B. GRAZIER
Consultant and author

Leading others is what the development of organizational purpose is all about.

To determine how well an organization has defined and communicated its purpose, I use a simple test. I ask organizational members what they stand for. Few people from teenagers to teamsters know the answer. Similarly, if they're working outside the home, most can't tell me why they work where they work.

I once asked a flight attendant why she worked in the airline industry. She looked at me with perplexity and asked if she could have some time to think about it. A short while later she returned and said: "I work to serve the customer." That sounded pretty good until I asked her, "Yes, but why?" She got flustered and said: "Because without the customer, I wouldn't have a job." It was a bottom-line answer.

The answer I receive very infrequently about work, but the one I find refreshing and reassuring is: "I work here because I enjoy my work. I can't think of anything else I would rather be doing." In other words, I am satisfied with where I work and live and, therefore, with myself.

The quality of the answers to these critical questions on personal and organizational purpose is often determined by the amount of effort an individual or organization has put into examining their reason for being. If we invested a fraction of the amount of effort in developing our purpose as we do trying to make more money, we'd all have a much better chance of achieving our desired results.

27

The see-through organization

Organizations are like families. They're made up of individuals. If those individuals are unhappy, chances are the organization will reflect it. If one part of a couple is under financial stress, the relationship may begin to fail. Corporate revenues may drop when a key employee loses his enthusiasm, is suddenly replaced or falls ill.

Organizations are not, as some would believe, inanimate objects. They are living, breathing groups of individuals. Thus, when the individuals within an organization lack purpose, so does the organization. Conversely, when the organization lacks purpose, so too do the individuals within it. Individual and organizational wellness are inseparably linked.

When we complain about how badly an organization has treated us, we are really complaining about the individuals within that organization. When we complain about government bureaucracy, it's the bureaucrats that we're complaining about. **If organizations are impersonal, they are made that way by the people who work in them!**

The reflecting organization

In much the same way that impersonal behavior is reflected in an organization, purpose (or lack of it) is also reflected. And, as always, that purpose begins at the individual level.

In business, for example, the individuals who make up the senior management group set the direction of the entire organization. Their philosophies trickle down and reflect on those they supervise.

Delta Air Lines's corporate slogan is, "Delta loves to fly, and it shows." If Delta's senior management group champions this, they must communicate it by their actions. To achieve the organization's purpose, Delta's employees must reflect these actions every day, in every way.

Thus, an organization's culture is determined by its employees, but is directed by its leaders.

The behavior of senior management, whether a parent, an older brother or sister or an aunt or uncle, is seen as the beacon for everyone else in that organization to follow. Where these leaders spend their time, energy and money is likely where others in the organization will spend theirs. [5]

The telephone test

A key component of a well-run organization is a well-defined and well-communicated purpose. A few minutes on the telephone with whoever answers it for an organization can often give us a clue to its purpose. Two recent corporate examples come to mind, but I could just as easily cite family situations with similar characteristics. Next time you call someone's home, listen to how they answer and how they treat you when you ask to speak to someone who lives there. It's illuminating.

One day, I called several corporations by phone and asked to speak to the president, whom I knew personally in each case. One company dealt with me as if I were a nuisance– they didn't want to know what I wanted, they didn't want to take a message and they brushed me off as quickly as possible so they could get on with what must have been "more important things." This, I later discovered, was a direct reflection on the president himself. He would not set time aside for a 30-minute appointment and cancelled the appointments he did make– even though he expressed an interest in seeing me.

When we finally got together he was a half hour late. His organization, I discovered, was growing in all directions at once, was selling product wherever and however it could, and was experiencing problems meeting delivery commitments and providing good after-sales service. No wonder! The organization was sales, not market, focused. All it cared about was the bottom line–the number of sales orders, the size of the profit margin, the number of deliveries–numbers, numbers, numbers. The organization was fighting fires to keep existing customers happy. It also had little appreciation for how its own attitude was preventing new customers from getting in the door.

This is what happened when I called another organization for the first time:

Organization:	Hello, this is Office Warehouse, your one-stop office shopping, Paul speaking. May I help you?
Me:	Good afternoon, Paul. My name is Mike Fuller. Would Harold Hogan be available?
Paul:	I'm sorry Mr. Fuller, but Harold is not in right now. I'm not sure when he'll return, but if you could hold the line for just a second, I'll look and see when he's scheduled back.
Me:	That would be fine. Thanks, Paul. On hold.
Paul:	Mr. Fuller, are you still there?
Me:	Yes, I am, thank you.
Paul:	According to Harold's calendar, he's due back at 6 p.m. for a staff meeting. Could he call you back then?
Me:	Thanks, Paul. I'd appreciate it.

At 6:15 p.m., long after most of the "working" world had gone home, Harold returned my call. I was so impressed by the way my call was handled by Paul and now, Harold, that I told Harold about it.

I have since learned that this president runs one of the more successful franchises in his company. He clearly knows what is important to the success of his organization–people–and he and his people deliver in spades. His attitude toward people affects their attitude toward others. Thus, there is a "trickle down" effect. Harold doesn't concentrate only on his bottom line: he concentrates on **who delivers** his bottom line.

And it isn't that he doesn't set financial goals–they are on public display at his office.

The contrast between the first manager and the second was powerful. One was entirely driven by results. The other knew what it took to achieve them–people. One focused on the bottom line. The other focused on who produced the bottom line. Think about it for a moment. Which organization would you rather be involved with? Which person would you rather spend time with? Which person would you rather be?

Mirroring the manager

Employees, I believe, are reflections of their managers. If you doubt this, look at your own position within your organization and determine whose attitude or behavior you are reflecting. Usually, it's your leader's. There are few people who maintain a positive attitude or proper behavior even when those who lead them do not. We are all influenced by those who lead us.

> *The true worth of man is not to be found in man, but in the colours and texture that come alive in others.*
>
> ALBERT SCHWEITZER
> French philosopher,
> physician, and music scholar

We're losing the numbers game

A recent study shows almost 50 per cent of middle managers are unhappy in their work. Because employees are influenced by their managers and middle managers make up the majority of those in organizational leadership roles, a simple extrapolation of this rate to all employees would be even more frightening.

The study reports that, compared to a few years ago, there has been a nine- to ten-fold increase in the number of dissatisfied middle managers looking for alternative employment today.[6]

This may not sound serious until you consider the fallout from this frustration. Unfortunately, the buck is stopping at the bottom–with the employees being managed. They, in turn, affect their co-workers and their children, and the whole unhappy cycle continues.

The role of work

To a large extent, the purpose of life throughout the world is vested in work. We spend more time at work than anywhere else, we socialize there and sometimes we even vacation with people we know through work. So, if we're unhappy in our work, as the study cited above suggests, how can we expect to create a satisfied generation to follow our footprints?

The importance of balance in purpose

Good leaders know implicitly what they want, what they need and where they're going. Yet most of us are out of balance. We either spend too much time working, too much time playing or not enough time at home. The imbalance this can create can detract substantially from our fulfilment in all areas. To succeed, we must either balance our many purposes simultaneously, or regularly alternate our focus from one area to another. This involves periodically concentrating on what is of immediate importance while knowing full well that we must soon refocus on other parts of our lives.

During exam or tax time, students and accountants are under tremendous pressure to complete work on time. Many work furiously until all hours for days and weeks in a frenzied effort to meet their commitments. That is their purpose. But, as soon as the deadlines have passed, the wise ones take time to recharge their batteries. This may involve time off or simply a quiet, contemplative period for self-renewal.

Rest breaks are difficult for some people to take. Most high schools and universities wisely schedule vacations after exam weeks. But, much of the rest of the world does not. It often sees no correlation between rest and return–either individually or organizationally.

At an individual level, some believe, equally erroneously, that their purpose is so central to their organization that they are irreplaceable. The question I always ask such people is: **What would happen to your organization if you got run over by a truck tomorrow?**

The answer, no matter how difficult it may be to admit, is, the organization would survive. Your family members would grieve, but they would somehow carry on. If you were a sole proprietor, your company might cease to exist, but at the very least, the world would keep turning.

As human beings, it is our nature to survive and adapt. It is how we have lasted for thousands of years in the woods. But without balance, the best purposes in the world will never be realized. We must not only work hard. We must work hard at balancing both our personal and professional lives.

Leading others

Now that you have a personal purpose statement, your next step is to develop an organizational statement. Again, an organization can be anything from a couple (a partnership) to a family, a business, a government, or a non-profit or charitable body of any kind.

Why develop an organizational purpose? Well, to play a vital role in something larger than ourselves–an organization–we must first know our role. Once we've

33

established our own personal purpose, we can use it as a foundation on which to build our relationships with others. These relationships could include those with family members or co-workers. A strong personal foundation, therefore, allows us to be more productive in our organizations.

Again, the process of developing an organizational purpose has three parts:

1. consider some thought-provoking questions
2. develop a list of key words
3. write your organization's purpose statement

You can do each of these by yourself or with others. However, experience has shown me that the benefits of developing an organizational purpose statement are maximized when a group of key players are assembled for the challenge. In a family, the group would consist of all family members, particularly those living at home. In a larger organization, it is impractical to include everyone. Thus, a small focus group representative of the organization should be assembled. That group **should not** include only "senior" management. In fact, it's often better if it doesn't. The key is everyone in the focus group should be key. There should be key support staff, key warehouse people, key sales executives, key accounting personnel–anyone who knows the organization well, who influences others and who has a passion for what they do.

In corporate organizations, you'd be surprised how well many support staff understand their organization's makeup. Some know it better than the president or CEO. An often overlooked person is the receptionist or the key employee in the warehouse or out in the field. They are particularly valuable if they've been with the organization for a long time. They tend to know everyone and many employees confide in them.

34

Aside from the above, there is one other recommendation for admission to the group. Each person in it should develop their own personal purpose statement. Although this is not mandatory, it is encouraged.

You'll need a flip chart, a white/blackboard or an overhead projector. Ask one person to record the minutes of the meeting.

Procedure

■ **Convene the group**

Explain the procedure for developing an organizational purpose statement. The goal is to develop a statement of 20 words or less. This is not a hard and fast number, but resist wordiness.

■ **Hand out a list of questions to stimulate thought**

For example:

For a couple:

● Why should others be attracted to us as a couple?

● What can we offer the world together that we could not offer separately?

● What are the key principles without which our relationship could not function?

● How do we see work, children, family, health, leisure, money and lifestyle?

For a family:

● Why should others be attracted to us as a family?

● What significant contribution does our family make to our friends, our neighborhood, our community and our country?

- What are the key principles without which our family could not function?

- What is the primary principle for which our family stands?

For a business organization:

- Why do customers buy our organization's product or service?

- Why do employees want to work for our organization?

- Why does our organization exist?

- What significant contribution does our organization make to the world around us?

- What has been the driving force behind the success of our organization?

- What are the key elements without which our organization cannot function?

- What are the major strengths of our organization?

- What is the primary principle for which our organization stands?

- What energizes our organization?

- How does our organization view work, family, health and leisure?

Your examples:

_____

_____

_____

_____

_____

■ Each person prepares a list of words that suggest their organization's purpose. (e.g., service, respect)

My organization's words to live by

_____   _____

_____   _____

_____   _____

_____   _____

_____   _____

_____   _____

_____   _____

_____   _____

_____   _____

■ Each person circles three words that most closely pinpoint the organization's purpose.

The three words that best describe my organization's purpose are

_____

_____

_____

■ Put everyone into groups of five. Each group decides through consensus which three words are most important.

■ The group writes a purpose statement no longer than 20 words. It should begin with an "ing" word.

My group's purpose statement

_____

_____

_____

■ Each group writes their statement on the white/ blackboard, flip chart, or overhead. After each group has presented its statement, everyone decides the best statement through discussion, elimination "wordsmithing" and consensus. (Consensus is not majority rule. It is a general agreement that the idea has merit. It may not be exactly what you would say, but you and the group can "live with it." The group, therefore, begins to approach harmony through understanding. This is not normally possible when "majority rule" is used.)

My organization's purpose statement

_____

_____

_____

(Depending on the size of the group, the entire process takes one to four hours.)

■ (Optional) Some organizations take the group's statement and give it to a volunteer committee or "strike force" selected from within this work group to fine-tune it to a final version.

What can you expect to see after developing an organizational purpose? Well, purpose statements can be as varied as the nature of the organization itself. For example:

For a couple:

- Helping each other achieve our individual goals in a mutually supportive, loving manner.

- Understanding we will both make mistakes, but that each of us has irreplaceable value.

For a family:

- Supporting one another in a loving way, even when we do stupid things.

- Knowing when push comes to shove, we will be there for one another.

For a men's or women's group:

- Challenging one another in a caring way to develop our self-confidence.

For a charity:

- Providing compassionate programs to improve the quality of life of those directly or indirectly affected by the ailment.

For Crestar Energy Inc., an oil and gas company based in Calgary, Canada:

"Building a successful resource company respected by our employees, their families, business associates and the community." (Strategic planning document).

For General Electric:

"Developing employee self-confidence and promoting simplicity to increase the speed in everything we do."[7]

For Levi Strauss:

"Satisfaction from our accomplishments and friendships, balanced personal and professional lives, and to have fun in our endeavors." (Adapted from the company's Aspirations Statement).[8]

Canadian Mountain Holidays, an adventure heli-skiing, heli-hiking company based in Banff, Canada:

"To challenge and enrich ourselves and our guests by sharing safe, world-class, wilderness, mountain adventures." (Strategic planning document).

Xerox:

"...Quality is the basic business principle for Xerox. Quality means providing our external and internal customers with innovative products and services that fully satisfy their requirements." [9]

The path of past purpose

In the past, religion traditionally provided an important purpose for our ancestors. When they worked the land, the family provided the most immediate foundation. The church supplied community support. Then, industry began to take hold. Factories, companies and cities sprang up, providing jobs, security and social centres. Another level of purpose and support was created. But when the world's economies began to falter in the Great Depression of the 1930s and most recently in the recessions of the 1980s and 1990s, governments entered the fray. Unfortunately, because of their own political and economic problems, governments could not provide badly needed support. To survive today and tomorrow, we will require a deeper sense of personal purpose and balance than ever before.

Present purpose

The church still exists and probably always will, although its role and impact is changing. The family unit–through divorce, separation and other stresses–is deteriorating. Secular organizations such as companies, governments and non-profit groups are getting smaller, not larger; leaner, not fatter. Job security is vanishing. There are layoffs and plant closures everywhere.

We can no longer rely on government, industry or the corporate world to maintain our lifestyles or catch us if we fall. Most of the conventional support systems are no longer solid. Increasingly, they are evaporating.

Today, we must build our own safety nets–and the fabric must last. For you, part of that fabric may be the purpose filled by your family, clubs, religion or the organizations where you earn your living. For others, it may not be. What will your net be made of?

Regardless of the fabric of our safety nets, to live our lives fully, we must look inward, not outward, for purpose. We are entering a new age of independence. To succeed, we will have to be more self-reliant. And we will have to know completely and emphatically **why** we are here.

If our only purpose is to work and make money, then we are treading on dangerous ground.

What we get from this adventure (of life) is just sheer joy. And joy is, after all, the end in life. We do not live to eat and make money. We eat and make money to be able to enjoy life. That is what life means and what life is for.

GEORGE LEIGH MALLORY,
British mountaineer

41

From purpose to vision

With an inspirational individual and/or organizational purpose statement in hand, the next step is to decide what you would like to be known for in the future. You now know what you, and your organization, stand for. It's time to take a look at what you and your organization hope to be remembered for.

Your second black door stands before you.

FOOTPRINT TWO

The Value of Vision

Dream lofty dreams, and as you dream, so shall you become. Your vision is your promise of what you shall one day be; your ideal is the prophecy of what you shall at last unveil.

JAMES ALLEN
Pastor, author

So there you stand before the door. Beyond it lies another forest of the unknown. The sky there is clear; the evening crisp. Through the keyhole, you can just make out the thin thread of a trail stretching off into the darkness.

Where we're headed

Just as in Footprint 1, this Footprint has two parts:

Part I: Personal Vision

    a. a discussion of the importance of personal vision

    b. questions that will help you develop your own personal vision statement

Part II: Organizational Vision

    a. a discussion of the importance of organizational vision

    b. questions that will help you develop a vision statement for the organizations to which you belong

Part I: Personal Vision

Like the previous Footprint, this one will present you with many choices. With your personal purpose statement in mind, your choices will be easier. By now, you have determined two things: why you want to make the journey and what you stand for.

Standing there is not good enough. To grow, we must take steps, but careless action is equally ineffective. Consider

44

how many of us tear down a new trail without really knowing where we want to go.

*One day Alice came to a fork in the road
and saw a Cheshire cat in a tree. "Which road
do I take?" she asked. His response was a
question: "Where do you want to go?" "I don't
know," Alice answered. "Then," said the cat,
"it doesn't matter."*

LEWIS CARROLL
English novelist

If we want to build a solid personal life and a solid organization, we must ensure that our foundation–our purpose and vision statements–are well thought out before we continue our journey.

The inner journey revisited

Deciding where we want to go (the first part of any vision statement) is the easiest part. It's easy because we can see our goal. It might be to achieve better grades at school, to attain a personal best as a salesperson, to improve our golf score, or to raise a family. Organizationally, it may be to boost sales, cut costs or expand.

Since these things are easy to see and evaluate, they are generally accepted by society. But although they provide us with clear objectives, they fall short in other areas. As electrical engineer Charles Steinmetz once observed: "Money is a stupid measure of achievement, but unfortunately it is the only universal measure we have."

Many of the people I've worked with have discovered that somehow, somewhere, they want more out of life than just running up the numbers–sales, scores, houses, cars, outlets. They want a long-term vision that goes beyond external things.

45

Your journey toward that vision has already begun with the development of personal and organizational purpose statements. They tell us **why** we want to make our journeys. Our vision statements tell us **where** we want to go and **who** we want to be when we get there. They're more than what we want to look like on the outside. That is relatively easy to envision. What we want to be on the inside is much more difficult to envision. That's what we'll be talking about in this footprint.

The value in values

People should know what you stand for. They should also know what you won't stand for.

ANONYMOUS

Who we are is a direct reflection of our values. Values are qualities that we want to reflect–like courage, integrity, enthusiasm, persistence and endurance.

Ideally, vision asks what we want to be when we "grow up"–not just in terms of a place, position or career, but in terms of who we are as people.

Think five, ten and fifteen years into the future. What do you want people to say about you and what you stand for? What do people say about you when you're in a room? What do you want them to say when you're not there?

Our own obituaries

We can choose how people remember us. Consider the story of a woman we'll call Mrs. Brown. When she died, the person who normally wrote the obituary column for the local newspaper was sick. So, the task of writing Mrs. Brown's history was passed to the sports columnist. In her research, the sportswriter could not find anything significant about

Mrs. Brown. She had never belonged to any associations, had not been seen much lately and no one could remember much about her. The following day, in desperation, the sportswriter finally wrote: "Mrs. Brown died yesterday. No hits, no runs, no errors, no one left on base."

What a sad commentary on someone's life. Yet how many people are really out there living life? How many are simply living their life out?

We should never forget that how we lived is how we'll be remembered. If you're anything like me, you might like someone to write: "Lots of hits, runs, errors and the odd home run. You paid your dues to get into the game and once there, played with honor, integrity, vigor and determination. You won some, you lost some, but you left behind a legacy of actions and ideas for others to follow. You will be missed."

After I am dead, I would rather have men ask why Cato has no monument than why he had one.
CATO the Elder
Roman statesman

Who cares who we are?

Some may argue individual and organizational results are all that matter–salaries and sales are the only line. Now, I'm just as results-oriented as the next person, maybe even more so. When I was at IBM, I worked furiously to get important accounts. I hated to lose a client to the competition. I believed what I had to offer was of greater value than any competitive product. And, I didn't just want the sale–I expected it.

But hold on a minute. This approach only takes us so far. In the end, I could point to good sales figures and a pleasant paycheque in times of recession, but I felt there was more to life than just getting the sale. I wanted to build more meaningful relationships with my customers. I came to value those who helped me not only deliver the sale, but also those who supported me through warehousing, delivery, installation and after-sale service. Their success was instrumental to my success and vice versa.

There is no way of knowing how those people might remember me today. I hope they'd say: "He was a good person. He cared about me and my contribution to the company and to his job." To me, those kinds of words would be worth millions—more than any sale.

The human cost

I wish when I was younger, someone had sat me down and made me write my own purpose and vision statements. I was too focused on my professional life then. I was consumed with the outer destination—the sale of products. I knew nothing of the value of the inner journey. To be accepted by my colleagues, I had to achieve the sales quotas established by my organization. The problem was, I never came to grips with life's real ledger. The revenue looked high, but the cost was higher. I lost touch with my family, with myself and with what was truly important.

I know what my purpose and vision statements are today. I think I would have been a more "value-added" person if I'd known them earlier in my life. Hindsight, of course, is 20/20.

The moment of truth

The moment, I think, when we start putting real value on things other than material returns is the moment when we really come to grips with what's important to us as individuals.

It happens when we put immeasurable value on our children, on our time alone, on a walk in the woods with a friend, or on the sound of the wind going through the trees. That's when we begin to grow–and know–who we truly are. Then, we begin to see others as they are. That's a **Wow!** you can't get from a paycheque.

One of the most interesting parts of this realization is that it can also increase the size of your paycheque. How? By creating a greater balance between the outer destination and the inner journey. There is real value in knowing the value of yourself. I didn't understand that until a few years ago. A theory called the "Pygmalion Effect" began to show me why.

The Pygmalion Effect

The Pygmalion Effect holds that our beliefs about people affect how they behave. So, if we feel someone is not up to a particular task, their chances of successfully completing that task under our leadership substantially diminish. We are the catalyst for construction or destruction.

When you were a child, did you ever tell your parents when you did something special–made a painting, tied your shoes, whatever? How did they respond? Were they supportive or did they just ignore it?

I remember a good friend telling me of his successful ascent of Alaska's Mount McKinley, the highest mountain in North America. Upon his return home, he presented his parents with a photo of himself on the summit. The caption read:

Love to you Mom and Dad. Because you never said, "You can't," I could.

49

If you climb a mountain, whether it is geographical, physical, financial, professional or emotional, and take a photo, what would your caption be? Would it reveal your parents' attitude toward you?

Write your caption here:

A note to my folks

_____

_____

_____

If your caption is positive, the base of your personal pyramid is probably strong. If your caption isn't positive, then this Footprint may offer you an opportunity to change yourself, and the world in which you live.

If the Pygmalion Effect is true, then something else may also be true. That is, **your attitude about yourself may affect your attitude about others.** Thus, if you feel good about yourself, you will likely also feel good about others. They, in turn, will feel good about you. Your self-concept will come back to you.

The organizational family

The Pygmalion Effect influences individuals and the organizations to which they belong. Managers in an organization affect their employees just as parents affect their children. Thus, if managers have a strong, positive vision of who they are, they can affect employees just as positively. While children tend to mirror their parents, employees tend to mirror their managers. But there is an added benefit to feeling good about ourselves: we are not as easily influenced by naysayers.

The late Bill March of the University of Calgary, in Canada, led the 1982 Canadian expedition to Mount Everest. During the expedition, there were four deaths, the worst avalanche on the mountain in a decade and six people left the team.

Some blamed Bill for the deaths. He was publicly challenged in the press by members of the expedition, but he stood by his decisions.

Miraculously, the expedition was successful in putting not just one, but six people on top of the world, including the first two Canadians.

I saw Bill make many professional presentations about the expedition through his eyes as the leader. In my estimation, he was an ordinary person. Yet he had extraordinary attitudes.

We live in a really interesting time. It's interesting because we're really short of leaders. We're really short of people who will make decisions and accept the consequences of them.

BILL MARCH, Leader
1982 Canadian Everest
Expedition

What struck me most about Bill March was not what he had done: it was what he exemplified. When he walked into a room, he had a presence, a force. There was something about him—not just charisma—although he had that, too. It wasn't just his association with Everest either. I sensed the guy was solid; he knew himself and through knowing himself, he better understood those he led.

As I see it, Bill's attitude was the essence of his excellence. Aside from his attitude, I repeat, he seemed ordinary.

51

Latent leadership

Do you know someone like Bill–people so sure of themselves you would follow them anywhere, even up Everest? If you do, then you know a leader. They may not be in a leadership position and they may not be charismatic, but they probably possess latent leadership abilities.

I believe no one can possess the attributes of an effective leader without having a deep sense of *who* they are. This knowledge helps determine what they expect out of life, their strengths and weaknesses, a deeper respect for themselves and for others and, above all, an enduring sense of high self-esteem.

Intuitively or consciously, leaders know themselves. They have, for whatever reason, survived the storms of life, and in the process, garnered a self-assurance that others immediately sense. If we have a solid self-concept–if we know who we are–we will become the kind of leaders this world needs. And, when we're gone, perhaps we'll be able to say what Bill said a few months before he died: **"I ate with the best, I drank with the best, I fought with the best and I climbed with the best. Shit, I've had one helluva life. "**

One helluva life

You can write your personal vision statement in much the same way you wrote your purpose statement. Think about this question for a moment:

■ **How would you live one helluva life?**

Think about your values, not just your activities. Values, once again, are qualities we want to reflect in ourselves. They include courage, integrity, enthusiasm, persistence and endurance. Take a few minutes now to think about them.

52

Procedure

■   **Write down some of the values in your mind**

My values:

_____   _____

_____   _____

_____   _____

_____   _____

_____   _____

_____   _____

_____   _____

■   **Circle the three values of greatest importance to you**

The three words which best indicate my personal values are:

_____

_____

_____

■   **Write a personal vision statement using the three values.** Consider what you might like to be known for in five or ten years. You may wish to shorten the time frame so you can focus on the person you would like to be in six months, a year or whenever.

- Limit yourself to 15 words. Again, 15 is not a number chiseled in stone, but try to stick as closely as possible to it. Start the statement with "To..." or "To become..."

Begin now.

My personal vision statement

_____

_____

_____

As with your personal and organizational purpose statements, your personal vision statement may evolve over time. Review your vision from time to time to see if it is still current. If it isn't, develop a new one. The essence of life is growth, and growth, of course, involves change.

The results of your efforts may look something like this:

- To be known as a cheerful person, one who has integrity and one whom others can go to for support.

- To lead a life others wish to emulate through my behavior in everything I do.

- To have an action-packed life, filled with adventure and seen as a journey others will want to follow.

- To leave the legacy of a visionary leader, known for mentoring others so they might succeed.

> *To be what we are, and to become what we are capable of becoming, is the only end of life.*
>
> ROBERT LOUIS STEVENSON
> Scottish author

54

Part II: Organizational Vision

The ability to adapt and adjust tactics while sticking to principles is extremely important. One of the biggest problems with CEOs is that they are flexible on principle and inflexible on plans.

> EUGENE E. JENNINGS
> American educator
> and writer

In the 1960s the Japanese had a vision of zero defects (perfection) in their manufacturing divisions. At that time the goal appeared unattainable. However, because of the Japanese initiative, by the 1980s and 1990s manufacturers around the world were vying for defect rates in parts per million and even, believe it or not, in parts per billion. Thus, although the initial objective seemed impossible, the very act of setting out toward the goal created the possibility of achieving it. Although the goal of zero defects has yet to be attained, the world as we know it has changed immeasurably because of the Japanese vision. That is the power of organizational vision.

There are other examples. In the late 1960s, Xerox's U.S. market share was more than 90 per cent. By the early 1980s, it had plummeted to less than 15 per cent. The decline was caused by complacency within Xerox and visionary Japanese competition that focused on customer service and quality.

Xerox, however, refused to wilt. By the late 1980s, it began to turn the tide in its favour. It adopted a vision called "Leadership Through Quality."

In explaining how Xerox came to this vision, David Kearns, former CEO of Xerox, noted in his book: "If we had a video camera and were here ten years from now and taped Xerox, what would it look like? What would we see?" [1]

55

The program permeated every fibre of the organization—from training and development to career progression, organizational flexibility, hiring practices and customer surveys. The goal was to win back the trust of the marketplace and regain market share. The program had a significant effect.

Procedure for developing organizational vision

Just as you did when you wrote your organizational purpose statement, re-convene your "Purpose People." Ask them to think about these questions:

- What values are required to have one helluvan organization?

- What do we want our organization to be known for?

- What do we want our organization to look like in ten years?

- What would our organization look like if it were an "ideal" organization?

■ **Each person prepares a list of words to describe what they want their organization's values to be.**

My organization's values

_____	_____
_____	_____
_____	_____
_____	_____
_____	_____
_____	_____

■ Each person circles three words that most closely pinpoint those values.

■ Put everyone into groups of five. Each group decides through consensus which three words are most important.

The three words which best indicate
my organization's values are:

_____

_____

_____

■ The group writes a vision statement no longer than 20 words. It should begin with "To..." or "To become..."

My group's vision statement

_____

_____

_____

■ Each group writes their statement on the white/ blackboard, flip chart, or overhead projector. When each group has presented its statement, everyone decides on the best statement through elimination, "wordsmithing" and consensus.

My organization's vision statement

_____

_____

_____

(Depending on the size of the group, the entire process takes one to four hours.)

(Optional) Some organizations take the group's statement and give it to a volunteer committee or "strike force" from within the working committee to fine-tune to a final version.

Here are some examples of organizational vision statements. Note specific products or services are not mentioned.

CRESTAR ENERGY INC., OF CALGARY, CANADA:

"To be a prosperous and growing company in which people share a common purpose, are proud of where they work and are proud of what they do." (Strategic planning document)

GENERAL ELECTRIC:

"We want a company where people find a better way, every day, of doing things; of shaping their own work experience, thereby enhancing their lives and their company."[2]

LEVI STRAUSS:

"When we describe the kind of Levi Strauss & Co. we want in the future, what we are talking about is building and affirming the best of our inherited traditions and bringing contemporary values and principles into practice."[3]

The all important alignment–again

The vision of the individuals within an organization should be aligned with the organization's vision, or they should at least be parallel. If an employee wishes to be known as a cheerful person, for example, then the employee's organization should see itself as an enjoyable place to work.

Is honesty an organizational value where you work? If it isn't, you may not fit into your organization.

Take a look at your personal vision statement. Compare it with your organization's vision statement. If they're similar, you may well be in the right place.

If they're different, you'll have to decide whether to:

- leave in search of another organization with values more in line with your own,

- adapt to fit your organization's values and vision, or

- decide if you want to try to change your organization's values and vision.

Shifting focus

With exciting personal and organizational vision statements in hand, the next Step is to decide how you're going to get where you're going–your focus. It will help ensure you're the person you want to be when you get there. It's time to choose, or break, a trail.

FOOTPRINT THREE

The Force of Focus

FOCUS:

- *The point where rays of light, heat, etc. or waves of sound come together...*
- *The starting point of an earthquake.*
- *To fix or settle on one thing; concentrate...*
- *To adjust one's eye or lens so as to make a clear image.*

WEBSTER'S NEW WORLD DICTIONARY
Second College Edition

Life can only be understood backwards;
but it must be lived forwards.

> SOREN KIERKEGAARD
> Danish philosopher and
> theologian

It is just before dawn. Ahead of you, there is the faint glow of the rising sun below the horizon. The air is still. There is a silence you can hear. Before you lies a single trail–not far beyond that, many paths shoot off into the unknown. You don't know which one to take.

For a moment, you panic. Fear begins to take hold. Your heart rate increases, your palms sweat. You wipe your palms on your pants. Just as you do, your fingers come across a map in your back pocket. You unfold it and suddenly, by the light of your flashlight, you remember where you are, where you want to go and why you want to get there. The pallor of gloom lifts and the cold grip of fear loosens.

It doesn't take long to determine which way to go. Your map tells you. Although there are obstacles ahead which aren't on the map, you set out down the trail with renewed confidence. At the first branch, you consult your map again and realize the options are many, but the choices are few. Most of the trails head off in the wrong direction. There are no trails that go the way you want to go. So, you take a compass bearing and dive into the darkness.

From the woods to the concrete jungle

In the concrete jungles of the urban world, it is easy to lose your way. Armed with a purpose and vision, however, you can begin to create your own map through the mayhem.

61

And, during those inevitable moments of self-doubt and confusion, your focus brings you back on course. Like the needle that always registers north, you can always re-orient yourself thanks to the power of your map and compass–your focus.

Compasses are unique. They are one of the few things in this world that never lie. Provided you keep them away from metal, they will always prove true, no matter where you are.

To be true to yourself, and to your organization, you must first know why you're in the woods (Purpose), where you want to go and who you want to be when you get there (Vision). A map is your purpose and vision. Your compass provides your focus. Just as a compass isn't much good without a map, you can't have a proper focus without well-thought-out purpose and vision statements. That's because your focus is a distillation of your purpose and vision.

What's ahead

Just as in Footprints 1 and 2, this Footprint has two parts:

Part I: Personal Focus

a. a discussion of the importance of personal focus

b. questions that will enable you to develop personal focus

Part II: Organizational Focus

a. a discussion of the importance of organizational focus

b. questions that will enable you to develop organizational focus

Part I: Personal Focus

The consequences of our actions in the "real" world of relationships, social acceptance, families, multi-billion dollar organizations, struggling small companies, stock markets and mergers can be serious. But whatever the arena, purpose, vision and focus must never be overlooked. If they don't excite and stimulate you, consider the following scene:

It is the 51st lap of the Daytona 500. You are roaring down the track at over 190 miles an hour, your car vibrating beneath you, the tires and engine straining. As you tear into corner three, Petty blows a tire moving into four and Yarborough takes evasive action toward the inside. You know Foyt is hauling down your rear-end on the draft. For a split second, any outcome is possible, even death. If you hit Petty, the race is not only over, but perhaps your career–maybe even your life.

Good drivers are always looking ahead. That's how they stay alive. To focus on the hood ornament, they know, is to taunt certain death. None of them have a death wish. They have a life wish–a purpose. They wish to experience all the things life offers–including the exhilarating sense of personal empowerment they get from being in control in a situation most people perceive as being out of control. Their vision may be the outer destination of standing on the podium drenched in champagne, or the inner journey of pushing themselves, their support team and their car to the limit.

Once in their cars, one of the things that keeps race car drivers in control is their focus. The world's best drivers shift their focus continually from their speedometer or tachometer to the car in front, to five cars in front, to a mile or more ahead. They look behind them in much the same way. They are continually looking for windows and doors–avenues of opportunity, or potential paths to disaster.

If you've ever watched a world-class stock car race, or a Formula One road competition, you know there are surprisingly few accidents. This has more to do with the skill of the drivers than the track, or the officials, or even the cars themselves. One of those skills is focus–the ability to concentrate on what's really important.

The driver's seat of life

Chances are, you are not a race car driver. But you've probably driven a car. Regardless of how fast you drive, the same principles apply. You know why you're in the car and where you're going. You focus on the road ahead–especially in bad weather. A winding country road on a stormy night can be just as deadly as Daytona.

If we don't focus ahead–to our future–we may find ourselves in danger in the present. If we concentrate too much on the hood ornament–the short-term view–and not on the road ahead, avoidable problems may become crises you cannot avoid. In an instant, we're in the ditch, or rolling, or...

America looks 10 minutes ahead; Japan looks 10 years.

AKIO MORITA
Chairman
Sony Corporation

64

The mathematics of magnificence

Let's look at how focus is related to purpose and vision. Here are some examples of individual focal points that we distilled from Purpose and Vision statements. Can you see how the creators arrived at their focal points?

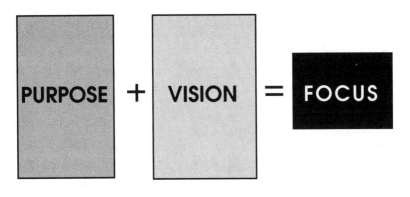

Purpose Statement:
Building personal renewal through programs building self-esteem in myself and others.

Vision Statement:
To be known as a cheerful, supportive person and one who has integrity.

Focus:
Self-esteem (for myself and others)

Reality Check Question:
To keep you on target, if the above was your focus, from time to time you might want to ask yourself: Is what I am doing, or about to do, enhancing my self-esteem and that of others?

SAMPLE 2

Purpose Statement:
Leaving a legacy of improved people and organizations.

Vision Statement:
To lead a life others wish to emulate through the behavior I show in everything I do.

Focus:
Role Model

Reality Check Question:
Again, if the above was your focus, from time to time you might want to ask yourself: Given my present and past behavior, am I a role model others will want to emulate?

SAMPLE 3

Purpose Statement:
Empowering people to achieve results through changing their work processes, behaviours and attitudes.

Vision Statement:
To leave the legacy of being a visionary leader, known for mentoring and coaching others so they can succeed.

Focus:
Building a legacy

Reality Check Question:
Through my activities with myself and others, am I building a legacy to be used by those who will come after me?

How personal focal points are developed

As you can see, your focal points are the one or two words that summarize what your purpose and vision statements have in common. So, just as before, start by writing down your personal purpose statement. Write your personal vision statement beside it. Then, try to determine what they have in common.

There is one other thing to keep in mind while developing your personal focal point or points–make sure your points and your words are not oriented toward the bottom lines of salary, material objects, place of residence, and position. These are outer destinations. Focus on things to help you deliver that outer destination–the elements of your inner journey. Again, to deliver the bottom line, we must concentrate on what produces the bottom line.

Write down your purpose and vision statements. What words jump out at you–drive you? Think about your focus. Write it down.

My purpose statement:

_____

_____

_____

_____

My vision statement:

_____

_____

_____

_____

My focus:

_____

_____

Remember, your focus is something so important it drives you to action. If you were a heat-seeking missile roaring through the woods, for example, what would attract you to the target, keep re-directing you around the trees, and cause earthquakes within you from the sheer excitement of clearing the obstacles? Look at your focus. Develop a question that from time to time will enable you to keep yourself on target.

My reality check question:

_____

_____

_____

Part II: Organizational Focus

Like successful individuals, successful organizations are clearly focused. This became very apparent to me when I began to study successful organizations many years ago as part of a personal research project. I read annual reports, books, articles and case studies about some of North America's most revered organizations. They included Hewlett-Packard, Levi Strauss, General Electric, Wal-Mart, Xerox, Federal Express and, most recently, Harley-Davidson.

These organizations all encountered obstacles, often huge ones, such as massive market fluctuations and major competitive threats. Like many organizations, they had purpose and vision statements. I read many of them, and those of other organizations, too. I discovered that these successful organizations had two things in common that other organizations didn't have.

First, they had focus.

Too often, companies trying to improve their manufacturing systems throw in a whole bunch of programs with no apparent interconnection– a work methods improvement program, a quality improvement program, an inventory reduction program, a cost reduction program, and so on. That can lead to disaster, because your employees become confused, threatened, and resentful.

It is far better to focus on a single, simple understandable goal–an umbrella under which all of your improvement programs can be linked together. In Harley-Davidson's case, the goal (focus) was " quality." For another company it might be competitiveness. [1]

The second thing these successful organizations had that the others didn't have was their point of focus. They focused above the bottom line. Although results were important, things that delivered those results–communication, training programs, the design of work space, coaching and facilitating leadership, measuring for the right results, encouraging simplicity, and inspiring the work force–were more important. Their compasses not only gave them their bearings, but also kept them on track. They understood the formula for future excellence: the distillation of purpose and vision produces focus.

69

*Semco has three fundamental values
(focal points) on which we base some 30
management programs. These values–
democracy, profit sharing, and information–
work in a complicated circle, each dependent
on the other two....* [2]

> RICARDO SEMLER
> President
> Semco S/A Brazil

Examples of winning formulas:

Here are some examples of organizational focal points distilled from purpose and vision statements. Can you see how the focal points were arrived at?

THE PURPOSE, VISION AND FOCUS USED FOR THIS BOOK

Purpose Statement:
Simplifying leadership material that positively influences individuals and organizations in how they work and live.

Vision Statement:
To become a landmark book.

Focus:
- Simplicity
- Personal/organizational
- Above the Bottom Line

Reality Check Question:
Are we keeping our ideas simple, are we always shifting focus from personal to organizational and are we keeping focused above the bottom line?

CRESTAR ENERGY INC.

Purpose Statement:
Building a successful resource company respected by our employees, their families, business associates and the community.

Vision Statement:
To be a prosperous and growing company in which people share a common purpose, are proud of where they work, and are proud of what they do.

Focus:
- Teamwork
- Simplicity
- Innovation

Reality Check Question:
Before we make decisions, do we consult people who will be affected (teamwork), and ask ourselves, is the decision creative (innovative) and will it make things easier for everyone involved (simplicity)?

LEVI STRAUSS

Purpose Statement:
Satisfaction from our accomplishments and friendships, balanced personal and professional lives, and to have fun in our endeavors.

Vision Statement:
Building and affirming the best of our inherited traditions and bringing contemporary values and principles into practice.

Focus:

- Balance
- Traditions
- Fun (enjoyment)

Reality Check Question:
Is my personal and professional life in balance, do I understand the importance of the culture that has built and nurtured my organization, and is my work fun (enjoyable)?

GENERAL ELECTRIC

Purpose Statement:
Developing our self-confidence and promoting simplicity to increase the speed of everything we do.

Vision Statement:
Where people find a better way, every day, of doing things; shaping their own work experience, thereby enhancing their lives and their company.

Focus:

- Simplicity
- Speed
- Self-confidence

Reality Check Question:
Is this activity simpler than the way it was done before, will it speed up service to the customer, and will my behavior enhance my self-confidence and that of others?

Some organizations have ingrained focal points so deeply that the points have become part of the culture of the organization. Most notably:

ALCOA

Safety, Quality and Capital Spending

> *By putting safety first, O'Neil (CEO)also encouraged employees to develop a larger view of their jobs and to start thinking more like managers.* [3]

COLEMAN CO.

Responsiveness, Results, Resources

> *Does the step improve responsiveness to the customer, does it improve results like profit and quality, and/or does it improve the effectiveness of resources like people and inventory?* [4]

The K.I.S.S. (Keep It Simple Stupid) formulas re-applied

I have seen many organizations needlessly complicate their focal points. They confuse and bewilder, rather than simplify and clarify, how the organization can get where it wants to go.

My rule of thumb is this: if it takes more than one short meeting to explain the purpose, vision and/or focus of an organization, the concepts are too complicated. If we don't keep it simple, we risk falling into what I call "The Value-Added Abyss."

73

The value-added abyss

I remember a consulting session with a major multi-national organization. Upper management had spent months developing strategic statements. They thought they were ready to pinpoint their focus. After a 90-minute presentation on the characteristics of successful organizations, I asked my group of assembled managers what their focus was. They told me the senior management had told them their focus was "value-added."

I got this terrible sinking feeling professional presenters sometimes get when they're put on the spot. I felt naked. They expected me to know exactly what that meant. Wishing as soon as possible to remove the egg from my face, I did what any normal, uncertain consultant would do to save face: I threw it back at them. I asked them three questions:

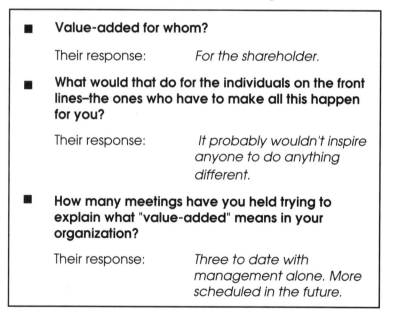

■ **Value-added for whom?**

Their response: *For the shareholder.*

■ **What would that do for the individuals on the front lines–the ones who have to make all this happen for you?**

Their response: *It probably wouldn't inspire anyone to do anything different.*

■ **How many meetings have you held trying to explain what "value-added" means in your organization?**

Their response: *Three to date with management alone. More scheduled in the future.*

I'd found my clothes again. I suggested they re-think their focus. I felt they needed a complete overhaul of their purpose and vision statements. That was the bad news. The good news was that it would take just hours, not months.

How to develop your organization's focal points

The process for developing organizational focus is the same as it is for developing individual focus. The first step is to write down the organization's purpose statement, and then, beside it, the organization's vision statement. Next, develop two or three focus points for the organization.

Make sure your organizational focal points, like your personal focus point, are not oriented towards the bottom lines of profit, return on investment or earnings per share. Focus on things that will help you deliver the bottom line. And, most important of all–keep it simple.

Hands on

Write down your organization's purpose and vision statements. Then determine what they have in common–their focal points.

My organization's purpose statement:

_____

_____

_____

_____

My organization's vision statement:

_____

_____

_____

_____

My organization's focal points:

_____

_____

_____

My reality check:

Look at your organization's focal points. Develop an action question to keep individuals in your organization on target.

_____

_____

_____

_____

_____

Back on track

Now we know **why** we're in the woods (Purpose), **where** we're going and **who** we want to be when we get to our goal (Vision). We even know **what to think about** most en route (Focus). Now comes the hardest step–deciding how we will actually get there. What equipment do we need to fulfil our purpose, achieve our vision and remain focused?

Ideally, we'd never enter the woods until we had chosen everything we needed. But life's journey has already begun. We're already walking down the trail and we're already in the woods. We can't get out of the forest, learn what we need and then go back in. Life is a one-way trail–forward.

76

Experience is the worst teacher; it gives the test before presenting the lesson.

VERNON LAW
Professional baseball player

We need more than physical gear to succeed in life. We need psychological skills. These include survival skills such as learning how to find a job, earn a living, deal with your boss, raise children, or put up with your parents. Our gear must also include key psychological tools such as how to handle stress, what to do when we feel lost, or how to fight fear, depression and self-doubt. Equally important will be knowing how to celebrate successes large and small and, something often overlooked, how to relax and recover.

Along our way through the woods, we face many obstacles. If we bring useful tools with us, however, we'll be better equipped to face life's challenges. Yet we don't know which obstacles we will face in the future. So, the physical and psychological skills we need to put into our pack aren't exactly clear. There are no hard and fast answers. The answers are grey and abstract. In short, they're "soft." And, they are hard to determine. They're the next Footprint– **"The Soft Stuff."**

FOOTPRINT FOUR

The Soft (Hard-to-Do) Stuff

When nothing seems to help, I go and look at a stonecutter hammering away at his rock perhaps a hundred times without as much as a crack showing in it. Yet at the hundred and first blow it will split in two and I know it was not that blow that did it–but all that had gone before.

JACOB RIIS
America's first photojournalist

The greater thing in this world is not so much where we stand as in what direction we are going.

OLIVER WENDELL HOLMES
American physician, author

Welcome to the woods. The day is dawning. The sun has just crested the horizon. With it comes the soothing warmth and reassuring rays of a fresh start–and new challenges.

As you enter the forest, you are still without a trail. You're navigating by map and compass. In many ways, you are still in the dark–we all are in life. We can look ahead, but we can't see what's ahead. We can plan for the future, but we cannot know the future.

The must-not-be missing link

Below you will see three overlapping circles. For a minute, I'd like you to imagine they are links in a chain. If you remove the middle circle or link, the chain is broken.

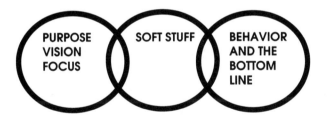

Now, imagine the link on the left contains your purpose, vision and focus. The one in the centre is the "soft stuff" and the one on the right is steps five and six in our journey–behavior and the bottom line. If you remove the centre link, the soft stuff, there is no way to get from the purpose, vision and focus link to the behavior and bottom line link. Again, the chain is broken.

The purpose of this illustration is to demonstrate the importance of the soft stuff. The soft stuff is **the** most difficult step on your path to increased individual fulfilment. It's also the step most people skip, because it is time-consuming and requires commitment. In this world of instant answers and quick fixes, the soft stuff is a really hard sell. It's a long-term commitment in a short-term world; a non-disposable element in a disposable society. It is a process, not a program. A process has no start and no finish, whereas a program has a start and a finish.

If you skip the soft stuff, the chain of success in your life will be broken. You'll see no improvement in results and your bottom lines won't change for the better.

For individuals, this is the most important Footprint in this book. If you read nothing else, read this Footprint. You can't skip it. You can't even skim it. It is central to your success. Bypass it and you will miss the forest for the trees.

The "soft stuff" explained

So what is the "soft stuff"? In its the simplest sense, it is all the physical and psychological tools you need to be successful. At the individual level, the soft stuff can be anything from clearly communicating your purpose, vision and focus, to improving yourself through self-improvement courses, recognizing the importance of personal space, learning to think positively, developing better interpersonal communication skills, keeping things simple to reduce stress, and selecting meaningful work and loyal friends. The list is virtually endless. In fact, to describe it thoroughly would require at least another book.

The "soft stuff" demystified

Over the years, because of its complexity, the soft stuff has become somewhat misunderstood. I'd like to demystify it.

80

Consider the personal physical and psychological gear you might need to become a better person. This may *sound* simple. It may not *look* like a black door. But wait a minute.

First, of course, you need to define exactly what a "better person" is. You won't find it in the dictionary. It's highly subjective. Therein lies one of the first obstacles you have to overcome in selecting your soft stuff–defining your goal. If you define a "better person" as someone with strict integrity, for example, how do you become such a person? Integrity isn't something you just pick up at the corner store. How do you develop this or other positive qualities?

We, as individuals, are all trying to better ourselves. So, what will we need to do it? Take a moment to think about it. Then, write down your thoughts.

> **Goal: To improve myself, all my life.**

Psychological skills I'll need:

_____

_____

_____

_____

_____

Physical skills I'll need:

_____

_____

_____

_____

_____

Other things I'll need:

_____

_____

_____

_____

_____

Behold the soft-stuff staples

Brevity, as Shakespeare said, is the soul of wit. In this book, simplicity is one of our goals. After years of experience, I have reduced the individual elements of the soft stuff to the seven soft-stuff staples listed below. These staples can be used in most areas of self-development. I chose them because they are the ideas I'm continually discussing with my clients. They are also the ones I discuss with myself.

I encourage you to develop and add those elements of the soft stuff that are applicable to your life. This book is not meant to be a finished blueprint, but a guidebook. The objective of the soft stuff is to discover the psychological and physical skills we will need to live more meaningful personal lives. This includes how we affect others. As we improve ourselves, we also improve the world around us.

For individuals, the seven soft-stuff staples are:

1.   **Broadcast It:**
     Clearly communicate your purpose, vision and focus

2.   **In-novate and Renovate:**
     Self-improvement courses

82

3. **Take a Time-Out for Time In:**
   The importance of personal space

4. **Talk Yourself Up:**
   Learning to think positively

5. **Don't Just See, Observe;**
   Don't Just Hear, Listen:
   Effective interpersonal communication

6. **Succeed through Simplicity:**
   Keeping things simple to reduce stress

7. **Live Like a Champion:**
   Selecting your place of work and choosing your
   relationships

Individual soft stuff staple 1

**Broadcast it: Clearly communicate
your purpose, vision and focus**

*Communicate, v., To make known; impart.
Impart, v., Giving to another a share of what
one has.*

THE AMERICAN HERITAGE
DICTIONARY OF THE ENGLISH LANGUAGE

After developing your purpose, vision and focus, tell others
about them. In doing so, you are much more likely to achieve
your goals. The logic in this may not be immediately apparent.
It wasn't to me until one day a few years ago when I decided
to run a marathon.

For ten years, I'd dreamed of running a marathon. The problem is, I'm no Olympic athlete. Yet, marathons have always captivated me. How could anyone run 26 miles, 385 yards? To that point in my life, the furthest I'd ever run was two miles. The length of a marathon was mind-boggling. But I saw others completing the distance and they seemed no different from me.

Yet they *were* different. They trained. They determined their purpose (to run a marathon), vision (crossing the finish line with pride) and focus (training). Then they decided what kind of training they needed (the soft stuff) and set about completing the training.

I told dozens of people about my marathon dream. Those who'd already run marathons offered valuable advice on training. Some actually trained with me. This I found deeply enriching.

Inspiration in action

If you want to feel inspired by a commitment, I mean *really* inspired, watch runners as they finish a marathon. Don't watch the front runners. Wait about an hour after the first arrivals to see something that will touch you deeply. It is the moment when the soft stuff, the investment of months of training, culminates in an extraordinary event for otherwise ordinary people.

There, before your eyes, men and women in their 60s and 70s, and boys and girls who have not yet reached their teens hammer, and sometimes stagger, home after a long, hard-fought battle. It is as much a victory of mind as it is of body. The fatigue is etched in their faces, but their spirit shines through. For a fleeting moment, the human spirit, usually invisible, bursts into visible brilliance. The runners whoop and cheer. They punch their fists in the air. Some sprint to the finish! Others just smile quietly. You can't help but feel it: the effort and discipline and tears and triumph. It is magic.

Alan Hobson, who has climbed on Mount Everest, says the greatest moment in his life wasn't on this climb. It was crossing the finish line of a marathon arm in arm with his brother. Why? Well, when his brother told him he wanted to run a marathon, they decided to run it together.

When they crossed the line, the achievement took on a whole new dimension. It was a shared achievement. Therein lies one of the values in communicating your purpose, vision and focus.

Grief can take care of itself, but to get the full value of joy you must have somebody to divide it with.

MARK TWAIN
American author

Running into reality

Marathon runners, artists, musicians, scientists, post-graduate students, entrepreneurs, managers–anyone who has achieved something difficult knows the value in publicly declaring their goals. A successful writer told me he'd spent ten years getting his work to the point where it could be accepted by a major national publisher. Finally, a publisher called to accept his work. When the call was over, he hung up and found himself alone. He cheered out loud, but the victory seemed less than it could have been. He had no one to share it with.

Shared pain is lessened, shared joy is increased.

CHINESE PROVERB

85

Let it all hang out

When we go public with our purpose, vision and focus, they go on the record. And once they're on the record, we're on the line; we're accountable not just to ourselves, but also to others. They become our external conscience. As we evolve, and our purpose, vision and focus evolve, the people around us also help re-shape our statements through their knowledge of who we are. Thus, these individuals have present as well as future value.

Something else happens when we selectively, yet publicly, declare our purpose, vision and focus. The moment we announce our intentions to those we trust, they become our support system. When we see them, they inquire about our progress. They will offer encouragement and even make suggestions. Although they may not always be there with us, they are there in spirit, cheering us on. This happened to me as I wrote this book.

Sometimes, because the world is filled with naysayers, those with whom we share our purpose, vision and focus may also discourage us. Those who do are usually a minority—not always, but usually. Still, it is important to take the risk of declaring our commitments. Why? Because, once we publicly declare our purpose, vision and focus, the whole can become greater than the sum of its parts—but not until we do. A dancer in performance can do things she might not do during rehearsal. The external influence of the crowd and the adrenalin it creates inside the performer can be the catalyst for moments of magic. That magic is produced by risk and commitment—the kind that comes with sharing our hopes and dreams with others.

Until one is committed there is hesitancy, the chance to draw back, always ineffectiveness. Concerning all acts of initiative (and creation), there is one elementary truth, the ignorance of which kills countless ideas and splendid plans: that the moment one definitely commits oneself, then Providence moves too. All sorts of things occur to help one that would never otherwise have occurred. A whole stream of events issues from the decision, raising in one's favor all manner of unforeseen incidents and meetings and material assistance, which no man could have dreamt would have come his way. I have learned a deep respect for one of Goethe's couplets: "Whatever you can do, or dream you can do, begin it. Boldness has genius, power and magic in it."

W. H. MURRAY

Who to tell

Tell everyone about your commitment to your purpose, vision and focus–broadcast it. The more people who know, the better. Your support system will become larger. Providence will also begin to move.

The very act of telling people about your goals does not guarantee you will reach them, but it does reinforce your resolve.

The merit in mentors

I believe strongly in sharing our purpose, vision and focus with mentors–people we respect and can talk to without fear of rejection. My ever-present mentor is my wife. I call her "my bride," not my wife, even though we have been married for 25 years. She has a fresh perspective on things–the way brides do. She also knows me, accepts me and loves me unconditionally.

87

Spending time with a mentor, whether they are your spouse, friend or colleague can be a refreshing process. I recommend getting together with one of your mentors every three to six months. You should also take the opportunity to have honest, open discussions with others–those people in your life who may not be mentors, but who are, nevertheless, important to you.

Pause for a moment and ask yourself who might support you in your present goals and dreams. Who amongst your family, friends, mentors or co-workers genuinely cares about you? Who needs to know what your purpose, vision and focus are? Write down their names–now.

Individuals with whom I should share my purpose, vision and focus

1. Names
2. How I will reach them (e.g., by phone, in person, by letter, fax)
3. Scheduled date of contact

NAME	METHOD	DATE

Call, visit or write to them. But tell them. Get the word out.

Individual soft stuff staple 2

In-novate and renovate: Self-improvement courses

In the previous chapter on focus, one individual determined his focus is building self-esteem–for himself and others. At first glance, self-esteem may seem like an abstract concept. It's like "becoming a better person" or "increasing your integrity." Yet self-esteem can be developed.

If you wish to increase your self-esteem–your belief in yourself–you might want to consider a course in outdoor adventure. (If this isn't up your alley, that's fine, but bear with me for a moment.) Whatever course you take should help show you potential you never thought you had.

Building self-esteem is one of the major objectives of Outward Bound, a program mentioned earlier. It is intended to improve self-esteem through adversity in the outdoors and includes such activities as rock climbing, ice climbing, white-water kayaking and back-country travel. In reality, the organization's name is something of a misnomer because it actually offers inward bound experiences–outer journeys that produce inner growth.

Other inward bound development courses available are: Dale Carnegie, Toastmasters, Alcoholics Anonymous and Personal Best. These programs push us beyond the present perception of our limitations. When we increase the awareness of our capability, our self-esteem is enhanced. Because these organizations focus on the self-esteem of the inner individual, I like to call them "In-novations."

What begins as an adventure into individual awareness has far-reaching effects on the world around us. Every time we improve ourselves, or master even small tasks, we are better able to assist others. Just like ripples on a pond, the positive effects of our efforts spread outwards in a circle of ever-increasing diameter.

89

What separates the winners from the also-rans

Even if self-esteem is of no interest to you, this may be: I have found that individuals who are among the world's leading experts in their fields are continually improving themselves through courses, seminars, conferences and conventions. Even if they are considered authorities, they are always building on their existing knowledge. They are always renovating.

While teaching at the University of Calgary I was always surprised that seminars on improving teaching were heavily attended by instructors who already won teaching awards for their inspiration and innovation. The good get better not just by being better, but by looking for ways to become better.

The famous French skier Jean-Claude Killy was no exception. At the world level, he realized everyone's skill and sacrifice was much the same. Everyone trained hard. Everyone got up early. Everyone gave it their best. So, he developed methods of increasing his speed by doing different things. By keeping his legs apart, he became more aerodynamic. By pushing off his poles, he could turn faster, and by skating into or out of a turn, he could improve the efficiency of his movements. The result? Three Olympic gold medals, one in each Olympic alpine discipline–slalom, giant slalom and downhill. At the time of this writing, the feat has yet to be duplicated.

What, then, is the key to continuous improvement? It's simple–look for a better way every day.

I'm going to take these self-improvement courses in the next six months:

1. _____

2. _____

3. _____

90

The reason I'm taking these self-improvement courses is:

Course 1. _____

_____

Course 2. _____

_____

Course 3. _____

_____

The skill enhancement courses I will take in the next six months are:

1. _____

2. _____

3. _____

The reason I am taking these skill enhancement courses is:

(Don't just say to improve the skill. Explain why it's important to you to improve the skill, e.g., I wish to take a woodworking class so I can start to develop the skills to build my own home or I wish to take a guitar class because music brings me joy.)

Course 1. _____

_____

Course 2. _____

_____

Course 3. _____

_____

Individual soft-stuff staple 3

> **Take a time-out for a time-in: The Importance of personal space**

The key is not the "will to win." Everybody has that.
It is the will to prepare to win that is important.

BOBBY KNIGHT
American college
basketball coach

The importance of personal space

The people I respect–the ones who have become my role models–taught me something I'd like to share with you. They taught me to spend time on my own.

This is not necessarily time spent meditating. It involves giving yourself time for self-reflection. Although everyone has their own personal time regimen, I like to spend a minimum of one half day per week entirely on my own. Here's a method you may wish to try:

Find a quiet location where you won't be disturbed. Pass the first 15 to 30 minutes in silence. Think at random. Don't try to focus your thoughts on anything in particular. Just let your mind work at the speed of its choosing. This mental warm-up should enable you to relax and prepare for the process to follow.

The next 30 minutes to an hour should be spent thinking about three things:

1. The Past:

■ **What have I accomplished in the past week?**

■ **What did I do well?**

■ **What could I have improved on?**

---

2. The Present:

■ **How do I feel about myself?**

■ **How do I feel about the work I am doing?**

■ **What is my level of self-confidence?**

---

3. The Future:

■ **Where do I need to go and what do I need to do in the weeks ahead?**

■ **What specific tasks need to be done?**

■ **What relationships have to be improved or developed?**

■ **Who will I need to contact for advice?**

93

If there is time left over, and there usually is, bring out all the material you haven't had time to read or fully examine since your last time-out. This can include magazine articles, books, letters, brochures, newspapers–anything you need to keep abreast of in your life or in your work.

Because I have an active interest in leadership, I often focus on leadership materials. Reading regularly keeps me up to date with what people and organizations are doing to improve themselves.

I am always reminded of the famous saying:

The grand essentials of happiness are: something to do, something (someone) to love, and something to hope for.

If, through these "time-outs for time-ins" you come in greater contact with something you truly love doing and something you are truly hoping for, you will have two of the three essentials. The third, something (someone) to love, you may have already found. If not, the presence of the other two will definitely speed you towards that something (someone) because you will have a much greater sense of who you are and what you want out of life.

In spite of the importance of taking time for reflection, most people don't. On the surface, time-outs for time-ins seem to take us nowhere. We're not physically moving toward the solution of a specific problem, hence we appear to be wasting time.

I see a lot of this kind of "exercise wheel" mentality in the world today. An exercise wheel, as you know, is a little metal wheel put in rodent cages. When the hamster, for example, increases its speed, the wheel turns faster, but the animal never goes anywhere. The faster it runs, the faster the wheel spins. The result? The hamster stays exactly where it is. The only real result is exhaustion.

94

There is more to life than increasing its speed.

MOHANDAS K. GANDHI
Indian nationalist leader

Time-outs are our moments to think, to unplug and to let the world go by. They allow us to recharge our batteries so we can proceed in a more efficient manner. They are not wasted time. They are time spent to ensure time *isn't* wasted.

Those who truly understand the concept of reflection have their mind wrapped around a powerful tool—one that very few people appreciate, let alone possess.

The men who have had the most to give to their fellow men are those who have enriched their minds and hearts in solitude. It is a poor education that does not fit a man to be alone with himself.

NOEL HILDEBRAND
Philosopher

Choosing your place of quiet contemplation

Okay, so you've decided it's important to get away from it all on a regular basis and to think about where you've been, where you are and where you're going. Sound familiar? It is. It's purpose, vision and focus all over again, but it's developed over a much shorter period of time.

Home is not necessarily the best place to take a time-out for a time-in. Neither is the office. There are too many interruptions. Weather permitting, an outdoor location is ideal—a park with picnic tables, a patch of grass or a stretch of beach.

I have found that coffee shops are excellent locations. Choose a spot at the back, or off in an isolated corner. Let the staff know you want to be left alone, that coffee, tea or juice would be appreciated from time to time.

Just as important as time-outs for time-ins are retreats that allow us to develop a healthy relationship with ourselves and with others. Time spent with spouses or significant others allows us to catch our breath in a lifelong race.

I will schedule the following half day each week to spend on my own:

(Circle one) M, T, W, Th, F, S, Su

(Circle one) morn. / aft. / evg.

I will consider the following locations:

1. _____

2. _____

3. _____

I will schedule the following personal renewal retreats for myself in the next 12 months:

_____

_____

Individual soft-stuff staple 4

Talk yourself up: Learning to think positively

I don't know about you, but I sometimes talk to myself. I often tell friends if they see me talking to myself, that I'm just having another board meeting–a self-administered counselling session. The trouble is, if I'm not careful, the thoughts I conjure up are apt to be negative. Like most people, I tend to dwell on the negative.

I have seldom lost sleep over positive things–except perhaps the impending arrival of Santa Claus when I was three. The most powerful book I've come across on the subject of positive self-talk is *As a Man Thinketh* by James Allen. It is a book I use continually. Although it is less than 65 pages long, I can open it almost anywhere and it instantly enables me to understand the power my thoughts have on my behavior.

> *Man (read Woman if you wish) is the master of thought, the moulder of character, and the maker and shaper of condition, environment, and destiny. Man contains within himself that transforming and regenerative agency by which he may make himself what he wills. Man is always the master, even in his weakest and most abandoned state....* [1]
>
> JAMES ALLEN
> Pastor, author

A famous corollary to this comes from William James, the American psychologist and philosopher:

> *Man alone, of all the creatures of earth, can change his own pattern; man alone is architect of his destiny. The greatest realization of our generation is the discovery that human beings, by changing the inner attitudes of their minds, can change the outer aspects of their lives.*

There have been many books published on positive thinking and I cannot recommend the most prominent of them highly enough. Dale Carnegie's *How to Win Friends and Influence People*, Norman Vincent Peale's *The Power of Positive Thinking* and Maxwell Maltz's *Psychocybernetics* are all classics. If your focus includes self-confidence, you need to read these books. To disregard them is to bypass some of the finest material ever produced on the matter of our grey matter.

So what's all the excitement about? The value of positive thinking has been recognized for decades. That's true, but sometimes the answers of the future don't lie in the present, but in the past. Looking backward can take us forward if looking back takes us back–to the basics.

Becoming your own private cheering section

I once managed a large downtown apartment building in a very difficult market situation. The downtown core was overbuilt, thus the supply of apartments exceeded the demand.

My job involved marketing the units, hiring and firing staff, managing building maintenance personnel, handling tenant complaints and attending to administrative tasks. I worked 12 to 15 hours a day, seven days a week. It almost cost me my family.

One day, I complained to the insurance agent in charge of the building. I said it really bothered me that no one was there to tell me how well I was doing. His response was direct and didactic. **"Well Mike," he said, "you get paid to manage. Part of your pay is the understanding that you've got to cheer for yourself."**

A light went on. From then on, every time I left work, I drove down the block, pulled over and stopped my car. I would think of three things I had done well that day. When I'd decided what they were, I'd drive home. When I got there, I usually felt much better about myself. As a result, I treated my family better too.

You hear talk these days about empowerment–enabling others to take charge of their situations. But the prerequisite to empowerment is self-empowerment. That's what positive self-talk is all about.

The next time I find myself thinking negatively, I will think these positive thoughts:

_____

_____

The next time I find myself thinking negatively about others or about how they have mistreated me, I will think these positive thoughts (about myself, others or the world around me):

_____

_____

Returning to the well

Like our thoughts, the people we spend time with affect us either negatively or positively. To make the most of ourselves, we need to spend time with positive people–especially if we're involved in a close relationship. I often work with people who require my energy and find myself devoid of energy after working with them. I have found I can re-energize myself by spending time with high energy, positive people.

Methods I will use to continually think positively:

- I will read these books/articles:

_____

_____

_____

- I will focus on these thoughts:

_____

_____

_____

- I will surround myself with the following energizing people

_____

_____

_____

Individual soft-stuff staple 5

> **Don't just see, observe; Don't just hear, listen: Effective interpersonal communication**

"You see Dr. Watson..." If you've read the stories of Sherlock Holmes, you know about Holmes's astounding observational skills. On one occasion, Dr. Watson inquired why Holmes was such a successful detective. Holmes's response was quintessentially him–direct, pragmatic and, of course, a trifle arrogant. He said:

> *The difference between you, Watson, and me is simple. You see, but you do not observe.*
>
> SHERLOCK HOLMES
> (Sir Arthur Conan Doyle)

Effective people have highly developed observational skills. They focus on what is happening around them, not just casually, but intensely. They don't just see, they observe.

To make good decisions, we must carefully observe the world around us. How good an observer are you? Do you focus on people when they speak to you? What are you observing about your surroundings, including the body language of those around you?

■ **Recall the last face-to-face conversation you had today. Write down as many details as possible about what the person was wearing.** (This may not seem important, but it indicates your overall observational skill.)

_____

_____

_____

■ **Next time you talk to someone face to face, what could you concentrate on that would enable you to improve your observational abilities?**

_____

_____

_____

Hearing and listening

In addition to excellent observational skills, effective people also have finely honed listening skills. Leaders may or may not be powerful orators; in fact, they may use speech sparingly. That is because they spend more time thinking and observing than talking. They don't just hear, they listen.

101

To communicate effectively, we must totally relinquish ourselves to those around us. In essence, we must become servants to our situation. Our sole objective is to be aware of their wants and needs, in order to ensure we listen to them.

■ **Recall the last conversation you had with someone today. Write down as many details as possible about what they said:**

_____

_____

_____

_____

_____

_____

■ **Write down as many details as possible about how they said it:** (their tone, their manner, their delivery)

_____

_____

_____

_____

_____

_____

In summary...

■ **List those people you can spend time with to improve your immediacy of focus, e.g., spouse, children, co-workers, mentors, friends...** (Choose people who force you to listen to what they say or watch what they do. Children can be especially valuable.)

● Those who will force me to listen more:

_____

_____

_____

_____

_____

● Those who will force me to observe more:

_____

_____

_____

_____

The key to effective communication

The key to effective communication is concentration. We need to keep our minds clear of anything except what is immediately at hand, and give it all our powers of observation. This goes beyond focus. **The extent to which we concentrate on someone telegraphs to them how important we think**

their ideas are. If we tune them out, we turn them off. We also deny ourselves the value of their ideas–ideas that could be solutions to problems we have at hand.

I recently attended a business seminar at which the speaker had successfully implemented Total Quality Management (TQM) in his organization. After the seminar, he was approached by many of the participants. I noted he concentrated totally on each participant with whom he spoke. He did not just chat casually. He actually listened intensely to what they were saying. One of the keys to his success, both then and in his business, was clearly that people went away from interactions with him knowing he gave them his full attention.

We can learn much about individuals by observing how they behave, even when they're "just" listening. We do not always have to see them at work to know something of their character. Our character, and characteristics, reveal themselves every day and in every way to everyone.

The Pygmalion Effect revisted

Remember the Pygmalion Effect in Footprint Two, The Value of Vision? It holds that our opinion of others directly affects how effective they are in their tasks.

The Pygmalion Effect also applies to effective communication. **If we believe others have worthwhile things to say, they will say worthwhile things. And, the more important we feel a conversation is, the more important the participants will feel.** What goes around in this world comes around–not just in our deeds and actions, but also in our thoughts. Although we may never tell people that what they say and who they are is important to us, they still sense it.

104

To see a glowing example of this, look no further than your own family. Did you grow up in a loving, supportive environment in which your parents truly believed in you and told you so? If you did, I would predict you are a well-balanced and successful adult. If your parents were not supportive, you've probably had a much harder time facing life's challenges because the cheering had to come from inside you.

I wish someone had taken me aside when I was younger, put their arm around me, and said, "You have the capacity to be great." It never happened. In fact, quite often, the opposite occurred. I just never got that kind of positive reinforcement–not through teachers, classmates, acquaintances or supervisors. In our youth, friends are more likely to laugh at our efforts and chide us for the way we look. These are the years in which family support can really make a difference.

Later in life, I eventually got what I yearned for from close friends. The support was great, but by then, I realized how much more powerful it would have been if I'd received it earlier. We don't need reinforcement tomorrow. We need it today. In fact, if we get it every day, imagine how powerful our tomorrows would become. There is majesty and magnificence in all of us, but we're not all properly nurtured.

Love does not die easily. It is a living thing.
It thrives in the face of all life's hazards,
save one–neglect.

JAMES D. BRYDEN

You may not love all those with whom you speak every day. I'm not suggesting you should. But this *is* a book about the business of life. In life, we have to value those with whom we come in contact. If we value them, they will give us value in return. If we don't value them, we shouldn't spend time with them. One way or another, they'll figure out what we think of them.

Individual soft-stuff staple 6

Succeed through simplicity: Keeping things simple to reduce stress

Even though it appears as though today's work force has become obsessed with time off, there is less leisure time now than in the Middle Ages, when one-third of the year consisted of holidays and festivals.

RALPH BARSODI

We live in a complex world. But it doesn't have to be that way. We make it that way. Every day, we are bombarded with more information through the media, our environment and our associates than our ancestors in the 15th century faced in a lifetime. It's no wonder stress levels have reached meltdown proportions. We've lost the ability to simplify our lives.

Or have we?

Any intelligent fool can make things bigger, more complex, and more violent. It takes a touch of genius—and a lot of courage— to move in the opposite direction.

ERNEST F. SCHUMACHER
English economist, author

Here are several ways to reduce the complexity of your life and eliminate habits that take you away from your purpose, vision and focus. Add to this list if you can—but to improve it, not complicate it.

How to swim against the current and still set a record

◆ **Simplification Step 1:**
Turn off the TV

Watch TV no more than one hour per night. You might choose the news, or light entertainment. Better yet, remove your TV from your home altogether–that's right–unplug it and store it elsewhere. You might be surprised at how you begin to relax in other ways, perhaps ways that truly do relax you–like talking to your friends, reading, playing games, taking walks or participating in sports.

◆ **Simplification Step 2:**
Play the sounds of silence

Turn your radio, tape deck or compact disc player off while travelling in your vehicle. Make a special effort to turn it off while en route to important appointments. Take advantage of opportunities to gather moments of silence around you–to contemplate, think, reflect, plan.

> *Mass transportation is doomed to failure in North America because a person's car is the only place where he can be alone and think.*
>
> MARSHALL McLUHAN
> Canadian educator, author

◆ **Simplification Step 3:**
Subscribe to yourself

Subscribe to magazines, journals and/or newspapers that focus on your purpose, vision and focus. In other words, if one of your purposes is to become the best parent you can be, then read about parenting and child psychology. I have found when I tell people my purpose, vision or focus, they cut out articles they think I might be interested in and send them to me. They also recommend specific books and periodicals. This saves me from having to spend a great deal of time wading through material to find the nuggets I'm after.

◆ **Simplification Step 4:**
   Journey spontaneously

Never underestimate the power of spontaneity. If you're passing by a park and have even five minutes to spare, go for a quick stroll. Stop at places you have never been to before.

A friend of mine taught me that the important thing is not getting from A to B as quickly as possible, but in the quality of the journey between A and B. Most of us are so caught up with "arriving" at specific destinations in life that we neglect to appreciate the journey. The tragedy is that "success" by most definitions is so fleeting, the sooner we "arrive," the sooner we depart.

Someone once told me: **"Live like today is your last day on earth. Plan as though you will live forever."**

◆ **Simplification Step 5:**
   Pitch the portable

Do you have a car phone? Use it only to call out and only in the car. It slays me when I see people at sports events, the theatre, even on the golf course, taking calls on their cellular phones. If the point of the recreational activity is to re-create, then why bring a phone?

108

◆ Simplification Step 6:
Drive around the problem

Drive to and from work outside rush hour. When I lived in Toronto, a city of several million residents, I would leave my home at 5:00 a.m., be in the office by 5:30 a.m., spend a couple of hours on my own, then drive out to my sales territory while everyone else was driving in to work. This personal schedule usually meant I went to bed early, but I didn't spend two to four hours in traffic every day just getting back and forth from work. I was usually home by 3:30 p.m. listening to the traffic report while many others were part of the traffic report. In most organizations, not much is ever done after about 3:00 p.m. So, you may as well be on your way home–ahead of everyone else.

Two hours of boredom and frustration in an automobile is neither an effective use of time, nor an effective use of your life. We are not made to sit and wait. We are made to explore and grow.

If you decide to change your commuting habits, remember to leave work early. Reward yourself for working smarter, not harder. Don't allow yourself to be pulled back into the mainstream.

◆ Simplification Step 7:
Stop early, and often

Driving on your holidays? Try rising early, driving until shortly after mid-day, then stopping. You'll get the best camp sites and hotel rooms, experience the least traffic and have the most restful drive. And, you'll have a chance to explore. If you find an exceptional location, stay longer.

I have the greatest respect for people who take five days to drive 500 miles, but who, in those 500 miles, experience 5,000 new adventures. Getting there isn't just half the fun–it can be **all** fun.

A simple application of simplicity

Everything should be made as simple as possible, but not simpler.

ALBERT EINSTEIN
American physicist

We don't need massive changes to make our lives more productive.

■ **These are two things I can do today to simplify my life:**

● at home:

_____

_____

● at work:

_____

_____

● at play:

_____

_____

■ **These are two ways in which I can simplify my interactions with others:**

_____

_____

■ **These are two ways in which I can simplify my life through my extracurricular activities, professional groups, Church, wherever:**

_____

_____

Individual soft-stuff staple 7

| **Live like a champion: Selecting our place of work and choosing our relationships** |

Take 90 seconds to complete the following three questions. They should help you focus on some of the ways to achieve your purpose, vision and focus. On the surface they may look simple, but they are amazingly revealing. Allow yourself only 30 seconds for each question.

■ **If you had four weeks to live, where would you want to live?**

_____

_____

_____

■ **If you had four weeks to live, what one major goal would you like to achieve before you died?**

_____

_____

_____

111

■ **Is there something you've always wanted to do, but were afraid to? What is it?**

_____

_____

_____

The answers to these questions should help you set some priorities in your life. If you answered you wanted to be somewhere other than where you are now, what plans could you make to spend time there in the next four weeks? What efforts could you make towards accomplishing your one major achievement? Could you make any strides towards experiencing the thing you've always wanted to do?

Life is short. Do the things you've always wanted to do as quickly as you can–today if possible. We could all die tomorrow. Today is all we have.

The time trap

Some individuals believe they're trapped in their jobs or in their lives. Yet no one in the free world works or lives where they do because they have to (except, perhaps, for medical reasons). **Again: No one in the free world works or lives where they do because they have to.**

We are all here by choice, and a little by chance. That doesn't mean we necessarily like the choices we've made, but we have made them. Often, the reason we live unsatisfactory lives is our fear of the unknown–our fear of the "black doors" we face. Some would rather stay where they are than risk the consequences of the unknown–but they are not champions. Champions know who they are and where they want to go.

Fear rules many people's lives. If we are over 50, we wonder anxiously how we will make a living if we move away and "start" again. If we are under 30, we wonder uneasily how we'll make a living when we're older. If we're "30 something," we fear being laid off or fired.

Wait a minute. What is our purpose, vision and focus? If where we are now is not fulfilling our purpose, vision and focus, then what are we doing there? Are we just paying bills or are we paying ourselves? Are we surviving or are we actually living?

We don't have to quit everything we're doing, throw our career out the window and immediately head off to do what we believe is more important. But in a gradual, thoughtful way we **can** begin to move towards living our purpose, vision and focus.

- **Is where I am now fulfilling my purpose, vision and focus? If not, why not?**

_____

_____

_____

_____

- **What steps could I take to change my situation so it could better meet my purpose, vision and focus?**

_____

_____

_____

_____

_____

113

■ **When could I start taking these steps?**
   (day/month/year)

_____

■ **This is my first step:**

_____

_____

_____

_____

_____

■ **When could I take that step? (day/month/year)**

_____

The next step in the woods

So, those are the seven Soft-Stuff Staples. Used together, they can greatly help you to reach your goals.

When I give seminars, I have discovered the energy level of participants substantially increases after just one hour spent developing personal purpose, vision and focus. Energy levels rocket even higher when the session is followed by choosing the best soft stuff to achieve purpose, vision and focus. For the first time, some participants know what they want and they have some idea about how to get it. The fog suddenly clears in the forest and there's a way through the woods. It is a fantastic realization. We can do amazing things once we have a clear understanding of who we are, what we want and how we can get there.

114

If you've taken the time to read this Footprint, you've taken the critical fourth step toward personal greatness. It will not be achieved overnight, just as we will not clear the woods for some time, either.

But now you are on the road to individual greatness and you are ready to take the next step. Ahead of you in the woods lie many challenges. Armed with the physical equipment in your pack and the psychological skills in your mind, you are now ready to meet those challenges.

It's your behavior, however, that ultimately determines whether you make it safely and successfully through the woods. Just as there is a strict code of behavior in the forest, there is also a code of behavior in life. If you know yours, and follow it, you will not only survive, but thrive. Your next step is action!

FOOTPRINT FOUR

The Soft (Hard-to-Do) Stuff

Part II : Organizational

*The soft stuff was the company's commitment
to our work force and the hard stuff was what
really mattered: (in our case) getting pants out
the door.*

*What we've learned is that the soft stuff
and the hard stuff are becoming increasingly
intertwined. A company's values—what it stands
for (the soft stuff), what its people believe in—are
crucial to its competitive success.* [1]

ROBERT HAAS
Chairman and CEO
Levi Strauss

Outside the factory, workers are men and women who elect governments, serve in the army, lead community projects, raise and educate families, and make decisions every day about the future...Children and grandchildren look up to them for their wisdom and experience. But the moment they walk into the factory, the company transforms them into adolescents. [2]

RICARDO SEMLER
President
Semco S/A, Brazil

Before we begin...

We are all leaders and managers. Some of us lead people. Some of us manage products, some services and money. All of us lead (and sometimes mislead) ourselves. Throughout this Footprint, whenever you read "leader" or "manager," substitute your name. Likewise, whenever you read "organization," replace it with whatever relationship, family, group, club, association, company or corporation is of greatest interest to you.

The history of excellence

Great organizations of all kinds–couples, families, clubs, associations and corporations, are built and maintained by extraordinary people. These individuals have a strong sense of who they are and what they want out of life (purpose, vision and focus). They also have the discipline to develop the systems (the soft stuff) that deliver the actions (behavior) necessary to achieve their goals (bottom line).

I believe we've reached a watershed in personal and organizational development. Cataclysmic change is upon us.

117

Where we've been

Those who cannot remember the past are condemned to repeat it.

GEORGE SANTAYANA
American poet, philosopher

At the beginning of this century, great corporate organizations were started and maintained through extraordinary people's relationships with money. Major financial institutions, steel companies, automotive enterprises and oil firms were built using this "human to capital" relationship. Leaders like Henry Ford, Howard Hughes, John D. Rockefeller and J. P. Morgan made names for themselves not only as inventors, but also as financial tycoons. The philosophy of the day was simple: pour money into an enterprise and surely more money will pour out of it.

During and after the Great Depression, the flaws in this philosophy became painfully obvious. The money ran out. Suddenly, something more than capital was required to succeed–indeed even to survive.

The post-World-War-II era brought the answer: technology. The ability to produce and distribute goods faster and faster satisfied consumer and industrial markets that were starved for product because of the Depression and World War II. With few exceptions, whatever was produced was purchased. This created more wealth, which financed more technology, and which, in turn, produced more product. It was a seller's market.

In addition to financial institutions, steel companies, automotive enterprises and oil firms, other organizations entered the fray and became great. These included computer companies such as IBM and Hewlett-Packard, airlines such as TWA and United, and electronics firms such as RCA and General Electric. This ushered in the era of high technology and mass production.

118

During the '70s, markets became saturated with products. Consumers had the luxury of choosing from the many services available. A buyer's market was born. Organizations realized they needed something extra to capture customers' attention. Marketing, advertising and promotion became more sophisticated, but they weren't enough. Organizations needed closer relationships with their customers. After-sales service and higher-quality products were born.

The Japanese were among the first to recognize this shift from technology to quality. They moved swiftly to capitalize on the opportunity. Twenty years ago, few people knew of Honda, Toyota, Sony or Panasonic. The words "Made in Japan" conjured up images of cheap, unreliable and poorly designed products.

Today, Honda, Toyota, Sony and Panasonic are household names. They have become synonymous with quality and service because the people who ran these organizations realized the importance of quality and service. Although some North American and European organizations also aspired to excellence, they were less successful because their standards were not as high. Now, thanks to a competitive nature and an unwillingness to roll over and die, organizations such as Xerox and Harley-Davidson are taking on offshore competition head to head and are doing well.

Where are we going– the relationship revolution

The next stage in the evolution of organizations is here: the relationship revolution. Great organizations must start treating everyone like their most valued customers. It's not enough any more to be good to the person buying your product. You must also be good to the people who supply you with components, who manufacture, ship, invoice, and recycle your product.

A recent article emphasized this point:

Another surprise: The new emphasis on value won't necessarily mean a cold-eyed focus on numbers and nothing else. The human element is certain to be more important than ever. To differentiate themselves from competitors, companies increasingly will rely on people who can successfully manage relationships– with customers, suppliers, subordinates, and peers... [3]

"The Relationship Revolution," as I call it, is not led by capital or technology, but by the one thing that drives them both–people. While this revolution may not seem earth-shattering, you'd be surprised how many organizations, particularly corporations, are still running (some are crawling) on long-outdated principles. And this phenomenon, sadly, is not just a North American problem. It is worldwide.

The roots of the relationship revolution are starting to run deep. In more and more successful organizations today, the importance of relationships and teamwork is starting to be recognized by some heretofore unlikely people–the controllers. According to a recent article in *Canadian Management Accounting Magazine,* these traditional "bottom-liners" will play an increasingly key role in the organizational world of the 21st century. The writer of the article advises:

> **To be a catalyst for change in your company, you (controllers) must have the following three ingredients:**
>
> *1. A Mission, (purpose, vision, focus) properly defined and clearly communicated...from the shop floor to the board of directors.*
>
> *2. A competent staff (the soft stuff)...*
>
> *3. Modern, sophisticated, user-driven, decision support systems. (customer focus and teamwork)* [4]

Make no mistake about it–healthy relationships are the hard reality of organizational success today. No couple, family, club, group, association or corporation can succeed without them. And relationships will still be critical in the next millennium. Without them, the organization that is our society cannot hope to succeed in the 1990s or beyond.

Looking out for number one

As I've explained in Footprints 1, 2 and 3, people who lead cannot expect their organizations to develop positively unless the individuals within them have high self-esteem and proper skill sets. The first relationship an individual must develop is the one with him/herself. High self-esteem will enable individuals to take the personal risks required to develop organizational greatness.

Team building

Successful organizations today have already learned the power of working in partnerships or teams inside and outside the organization. Total Quality Management (TQM) nurtures this team relationship: with employees to find better ways to solve problems and take advantage of opportunities, with suppliers to ensure high-quality products and proper delivery schedules and with customers to ensure the organization is producing what the customer needs. No organization of any kind can succeed today without these strategic alliances.

The foundation of the soft stuff, therefore, has two levels of relationships:

1. personal relationships and

2. the power of working in teams or strategic alliances.

What exactly is"the soft stuff"?

When I talk about "the soft stuff," leaders from presidents to parents look at me like I'm soft in the head. Although the term is now widely accepted in management, it is still misunderstood, even in business circles. Softness, after all, is not something that's usually important to hard-nosed, bottom-line-oriented leaders. They want hard facts, right answers and fast results.

In a sentence, the soft stuff is, as we've already learned, the physical and psychological equipment you and those around you (hence the importance of relationships) need to bridge the gap between organizational purpose, vision, focus and bottom lines. It enables you, through them and with them, to actually implement your purpose, vision, focus and thus achieve better results. The soft stuff is everything from training and development to communication, positive living/working conditions and the creative measurement of performance. As Xerox defined it:

> *(there are) six elements necessary to become a total quality company: reward and recognition; training; standards and measures; communications; a transition team; and appropriate senior management behavior...* [5]
>
> DAVID KEARNS
> Former CEO, Xerox

Done properly, the soft stuff will align individuals to the purpose, vision and focus of an organization. In short, everyone (or almost everyone) should be able to march in the right direction, in the right way, for the right reasons–their own individual reasons.

Although the soft stuff isn't hard to understand, it is hard to choose. If you want your family to be known as one that is caring, for example, what are the keys to achieving that objective? Do you need improved internal communication, a

122

better nurturing of good values, some kind of reward system for caring behavior, or all of the above? The list of possible ways to improve a corporate organization's care for its customers is just as endless. Therein lies the major difficulty of the soft stuff–deciding where to begin.

The soft stuff in action

I'd like to begin with a story. It will help us to choose those elements of the soft stuff applicable to most situations.

A friend of mine was recently handed the reigns of an inefficiently operated state-of-the-art bottling plant. The organization was in trouble. Market share was shrinking. The plant was seriously under capacity and most employees were unhappy. The plant was operating at 30-per-cent efficiency and quality standards ranked the facility in the bottom 5 of 30 similar operations in the country.

Instead of attacking the problem from a financial perspective, my friend attacked it from the human side. First, he observed there were several entrances into the plant, but only one for plant staff. It was staffed by security guards who demanded identification and who even carried out the occasional exit search. All employees punched in and out on time clocks.

During his first walk through the building, my friend also noticed the doors to the executive offices were equipped with automatic door closers, which were electronically activated from nearby managers' desks. Employees were rarely allowed into either the executive offices or the oak-panelled executive conference room, which was furnished with a mahogany table and pigskin chairs and was rarely used except for "high level" management meetings.

Shop floor workers were never permitted to interact with personnel from marketing or administration. The only reason managers ever appeared on the shop floor was

123

to discipline workers. Because of this, employees usually hid during management visits. Worst of all, there was no strategic plan.

Within one month...

Within 30 days, my friend ordered the removal of the security guards, took out the time clocks and put employees on a work and security honour system. He opened access to the plant from all entrances, removed the automatic door closers in the executive offices and held all meetings with his door open. He invited plant staff to tour the executive offices and opened the boardroom to all staff for meetings. He also insisted that all management staff make regular visits to the plant floor. He personally visited the plant whenever possible, and spoke openly with staff. Finally, he initiated planning sessions with his management team that eventually involved everyone from shop floor workers to front line supervisors.

Within six months...

Within six months, he was holding two-day leadership seminars during which strategic plans were revisited and everyone was asked for their ideas on how to implement the plans. Once the plans were approved, monthly day-long seminars were held for follow-up, training and development. He personally attended all training sessions, and encouraged employees to take pride in themselves, their organization and their products.

Employees responded quickly and enthusiastically. They began to think like marketers. Some went so far as to improve the appearance of their product's supermarket displays. This gave their organization a better image and improved sales.

124

My friend encouraged team decision-making. When the company was looking for more efficient ways to organize the plant, he asked for employee input on the physical layout of the facility. A plant model was placed on the shop floor, and employees were encouraged to make suggestions.

Initially, the model was to stay on the shop floor for a week. Employees asked that it be left longer. For two months, during breaks and before and after work, workers fine tuned the model. The plant was refitted and reorganized to incorporate many of their suggestions.

Employees began to assume leadership in many areas. With no direction whatsoever from management, they initiated a new dress code. It was not approved until all staff gave their input. My friend began regular visits to distant branches to communicate the corporation's vision and goals. These sessions took on a town hall meeting atmosphere. Miscommunications were corrected. Employee morale increased. Finally, company officials began looking for new, non-competing product lines to increase plant utilization.

Within 18 months...

Within 18 months, the plant won the organization's top national quality award and became the most improved plant in North America. It increased its efficiency from 30 to almost 90 per cent. It also placed sixth among plants at the corporation's worldwide level. Market share was maintained despite intense competition and plant utilization improved with the introduction of new product lines. The boardroom became a regular employee luncheon/meeting room.

Keys to this successful implementation of the soft stuff

- Small, immediate and highly visible management changes signalled a re-birth for the organization. By removing security guards, increasing plant access, eliminating time clocks and opening executive offices, trust levels between shop workers and management improved.

- A reduction in the emphasis on stratification and hierarchy of all employees increased the opportunity for communication–upwards and downwards.

- The development of a strategic plan gave the organization a guide from which to operate and offered everyone the opportunity to contribute to the company's future.

- Everyone found a focus: they became marketers.

- The open offices, new dress code and plant re-organization reinforced the team decision-making process.

In review

Notice that the soft-stuff decisions did not take place in any particular sequence. And they were all applicable to relationships, families and clubs as well as to corporations. The mix will vary according to every organization and its challenges, but there are some staples common to the process—the "right stuff" for organizations.

The right stuff

While attending graduate business school in the late '60s, I was inundated with case studies about organizations in financial trouble. As a student, my goal was to figure out some way to turn the organizations around.

When I became a university business professor a few years later, I found myself doing exactly the same thing: teaching students how to turn trouble into triumph. Then, around 1980, I attended an M.B.A. class at Harvard Business School. The professor presented the case study of a very successful company called Lincoln Electric, of Cleveland, Ohio. Lincoln Electric, which specialized in manufacturing and selling electric welding equipment, had become the world's largest manufacturer and distributor of arch welding products. I was immediately struck by the company's ability to take human behavior principles and put them into practice successfully. The kicker for me was the realization that the keys to Lincoln Electric's success were directly transferrable to many other organizations.

For the first time, I began to reconsider the wisdom of my education–and my teaching. Why, I began to ask, were we always focusing on organizations in trouble? Why not concentrate on teaching people about successful organizations?

Where we're going

Just as with individual soft stuff, this chapter will discuss seven "soft-stuff staples" for organizational excellence. They are by no means all of the elements you can bring to bear on your situation, but in my experience, they are the ones most often needed–and sometimes the ones most often forgotten. In light of the bottling plant case, see if any of these make sense to you.

127

The seven soft-stuff staples for organizations are:

1. **Spread the word:**
   Clearly and confidently communicate your organization's purpose, vision and focus

2. **Arm the troops:**
   Use the tools of training and development

3. **Build bridges, not walls:**
   Design living/working space that actually works

4. **Lead, follow or get out of the way:**
   Recognize the roles of a leader

5. **The right ruler:**
   Measure creatively and meaningfully

6. **Keep it simple stupid:**
   Can the complexity

7. **Passion, power and pizazz:**
   Inspire others

How to use the staples

The most common mistake made by the vast majority of leaders in working with the soft stuff is to bypass it and go directly from planning to continuous improvement. They do this because:

- They don't understand the critical importance of the soft stuff in delivering an organization's purpose, vision and focus;

- the soft stuff takes time, effort and money; and

- they are impatient.

So, instead of doing this

...they try doing this:

The problem with the second approach should be immediately obvious, but thousands, in fact millions of leaders miss it every year. The point is this: **You can't get from planning to continuous improvement without going through the soft stuff. I repeat: You can't get from planning to continuous improvement without going through the soft stuff.**

Slowly, some forward-thinking organizations are waking up to the important effect of the soft stuff on the bottom line. Some corporations, like Levi Strauss and Xerox, are even building it into their criteria for advancement.

> *One-third of a manager's raise, bonus and other financial rewards depends on their ability to manage aspirationally (according to values and the soft stuff)...The point is, it's big enough to get people's attention. It's real. There's money attached to it. Giving people tough feedback and a low rating on aspirational management means improvement is necessary no matter how many pants they got out the door. Promotion is not in the future unless you improve.[6]*

So: don't even think of skipping the soft stuff.

Beware the simple answer to a complex question

Some individuals oversimplify why they think soft stuff works. In any individual or organizational activity, caution must be taken not to attribute results to factors that may not be the entire reason for the results. When a family is happy, for example, I've heard observers exclaim: "No wonder they're happy: they're financially secure." In the case of corporations,

I hear: "No wonder they're successful, they have employee stock option purchase plans." But, the achievements of successful organizations are the result of many factors, all present and going on at the same time and each interacting with one another. This process is what contributes to an organization's overall wholeness or health.

So, the flaws in these arguments are glaring. Yet they underscore another important point about the soft stuff–it brings results. And, you will get even better results if you use all seven staples. If you think you can achieve long-term, enduring results by using just one staple, your rationale (I'm sorry to say), is equally flawed. It's like the misconception that holds that a university degree entitles you to a job. It doesn't–knowledge, talent, persistence and passion get you a job. A solid understanding of purpose, vision, focus, the soft stuff, brilliant behavior and great bottom lines should enable you to achieve excellence in that job–and build a career.

Organizational soft-stuff staple 1: Spread the word

> **Clearly and confidently communicate your organization's purpose, vision and focus**

Many leaders become frustrated soon after strategic planning sessions because they see no immediate change in the way the members of their organization behave. As a result, it's back to business as usual.

It is a sad fact that few strategic plans are actually implemented. These are the primary reasons:

- Those who actually put the plan into action are not involved in the planning process. The implementers, therefore, have no say in the plan and have had no opportunity to shape it into "their" vision of how they can accomplish the tasks demanded.

131

- Communication between the designers of the plan and those who actually put the plan into action is weak.(Remember how the bottling plant employees were not even consulted about the floor plan of their factory until new management made communication a way of life. And don't forget the results!)

- The strategic plan is poorly written. It is either detailed and complex, contains too many new initiatives, or simply lacks focus. (One of my clients equates focusing his plan with determining war targets so his employees can act like "heat-seeking missiles.")

- There is a lack of proper follow-up to ensure the plan is actually put into action. (In the bottling plant example, training and communication was not a short-term program, it was a focused, continuous process.) [7]

Pinpointing problems in your plan

Regardless of the nature of your organization, the following questions should help you pinpoint potential flaws in the communication of your strategic plan. Take a moment to fill in the blanks.

■ **In summary, what is your organization's strategic plan?**

_____

_____

_____

Discussion:

If you don't have a plan, you need one. If your plan takes more than five lines to describe, it's probably too complex.

- **Can you understand the strategic plan as it's written?**

| Circle one: | **Yes   No   Sort of** |

Discussion:

If your answer isn't a clear "yes," your plan may need revision. If your plan is unclear, don't implement it. If you try, it will just lead to frustration and failure. Start from a position of strength.

- **What are your strategic plan's three primary points of focus?**

1. _____

2. _____

3. _____

Discussion:

If you don't have three points of focus, you need them. If you've got more than three, chances are the plan is too scattered. Can you understand the points of focus? Avoid nebulous words like "value-added."

- **Who developed your strategic plan?**

  • Senior Leaders

_____

_____

_____

- **Other Leaders**

_____

_____

_____

- **Informal Leaders**

_____

_____

_____

- **Others**

_____

_____

_____

Discussion:

If any of your lines are blank, your planning group may be missing some important people. If you're weighted heavily in one area, that's also a potential warning sign. Obviously, you can't include everyone, but you should include someone from your organization's key groups. I call these people the "informal leaders" or "locker room coaches." In a corporation, it could be a receptionist. In a family, an informal leader might be a close family friend.

■ **Specifically, how is the strategic plan being communicated to everyone in your organization?**

_____

_____

_____

Discussion:

Haphazard or implied communication is not enough. Remember the old game in which ten people sat in a circle? The first person whispered one sentence into the ear of the person next to them and then they, in turn, whispered what they thought they heard into the ear of the person next to them? By the time it got to the last person, the original sentence made no sense whatsoever.

When it comes to organizations, this description can be frighteningly accurate. Don't get caught in the circle of miscommunication. It is better to communicate face to face with ten people at once than to rely on each of those people to communicate with each other.

If your organization is large, consider having each department develop their own strategic plans using the main plan as a model. Start by forming a communications group. Brief the members of the group either individually or collectively on the plan. Then have each member, in turn, tell you what they understand the plan to be and how they might communicate it. When you are confident everyone is "reading from the same page," send them out to spread the word on your behalf. But don't leave it there–follow it up to see how they're doing.

■ **How often is your strategic plan revisited with members of your organization?**

_____

_____

_____

Discussion:

The frequency with which a strategic plan is revisited has dramatic impact on its effectiveness. The reason is simple—change. Change in the environment, the industry, the economy, the market or even in the organization itself can make the most well-designed strategic plan obsolete overnight.

The process of revisiting your plan does not have to be time-consuming. Often, it can be done in half a day. It is erroneous to believe strategic plans always take years to develop and just as long to revise. I believe if you cannot revise (if necessary) your plan in under one day, your plan is too complex, your methods are too inefficient, or your planning group may need to be re-assembled with different players.

I recommend revisiting the plan about once a month. If you wait any longer, it may become too antiquated.

There are no hard and fast rules for the frequency with which a strategic plan must be revisited. Do it as often as you feel necessary—but don't just shelve it and forget about it.

Failing to plan, and act on the plan, is planning to fail.

ANONYMOUS

136

■ On a scale of 1 to 10 (10 is excellent), how successful has your organization been in putting your strategic plan into action?

Circle one:

1   2   3   4   5   6   7   8   9   10

Discussion:

This question, of course, is the meat of the matter. If you rank your organization at six or less, it's time to look at either the plan or its delivery methods. If you score seven or eight, look for ways to improve. If you score 9 or 10, celebrate your success–but don't take it for granted. You must continue to work hard to keep your high rating.

■ In view of your answers to the above questions, what are the current roadblocks to effectively communicating and implementing your plan?

_____

_____

■ What do you intend to do about knocking down these roadblocks?

_____

_____

All talk can be a lot of action

When it comes right down to it, the core of strategic planning–once the plan's been successfully developed–is communication. By far the biggest problem facing individuals in organizations today is their inability to communicate meaningfully among themselves.

> *Internal communications—talk back and forth within the organization, up and down the hierarchy–may well be more important to a company's success than external communications...It's the free flow of information inside the company that enables you to identify and attack problems fast...*[8]

If there is a struggle to effectively communicate within an organization, imagine how difficult it must be for persons outside the organization to communicate with those people inside. If signals are unclear inside, they're bound to be more mixed up outside the organizational community.

Discussion:

Dr. Walter Wright, president of Vancouver's Regent College, one of Canada's largest theological seminaries, writes a personally typed note to each of his immediate employees at least once a year. In it, he explains how he feels they have communicated and implemented the organization's strategic plan over the last year. He also reviews his past expectations of them and how well they have been met. While the note is heartfelt, it is also instructional. Here's one:

Dear_____:

We have come to the end of your first year working in support of the President's office and the faculty. You have been a wonderful addition to the team. I have appreciated the quality of the work you have undertaken and the spirit with which you have contributed to the College community.

You are a good writer and you follow through on the assignments handed to you. I have especially appreciated the way you identify needs at the College and put yourself in a place to address those needs. The current Teaching Assistant assignment is a reflection of that. Already you have given structure and direction to an important student and faculty aid program. I hear nothing but praise for your efforts in this area.

Your warmth and friendliness also contribute to creating the kind of environment I would like to see characterize our office. In addition I have benefited personally from your knowledge of Vancouver and some of the "Canadian political" aspects still strange to a Southern Californian.

Thank you.

Sincerely,

Walter C. Wright, Jr.
President, Regent College

The objective of these and other such practices is clear: communicate organizational purpose, vision and focus, but do it in a personal and positive way. There's no need for formal, impersonal directives from parents, partners, the president, head office, or "them." All communication should take place on a face-to-face or one-to-one basis. In large organizations, this may seem impossible, but it actually isn't. It's a question of pinpointing the leaders in the organization, communicating with them and then having them, in turn, contact those whom they lead. Once again, relationships are key.

Communication–or lack thereof

I wish I had a discount gas coupon for every time people tell me members of their organization don't communicate very well with one another. If I did, I'd never pay for gas. I hear tales of communications woes from family members, representatives of clubs and especially from corporate and government employees.

The number one complaint from teenagers and spouses to presidents and CEOs is that no one is listening to them. I hear leaders say: "How many times do I have to tell them to do something before they go and do it?" I hear employees say: "He [she] turns a deaf ear to anything I have to say. Why won't he [she] just listen to me?"

Fewer than half the employees polled in a 1990 study by Towers Perrin (an international survey organization) believe management is aware of the problems they face. And in the Hays Group's research (a management consultant firm) covering one million employees in over 2,000 organizations only 34% responded favorably to questions about how well their company listens to them.[9]

When communication is poor within an organization, people inside and outside stop trusting each other. Then, a very destructive cycle begins:

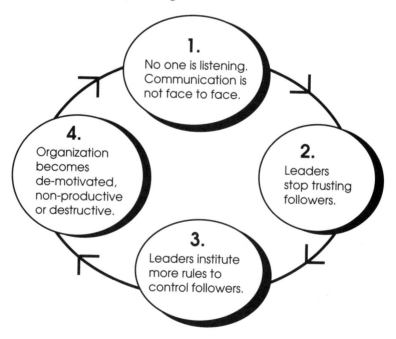

To succeed, organizations must reverse the cycle:

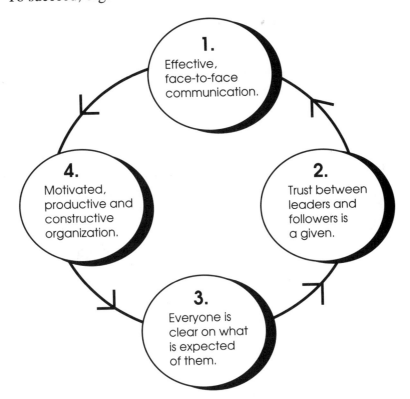

Listen to the sound of success

The most important element of productive communication is the ability to listen effectively.

Listening is far more than keeping your mouth shut or nodding your head and saying, "uh huh." It is the art of hearing what's being said, understanding it, analyzing it and then asking an intelligent question. This either improves the quality of the conversation from the other person's point of view or simply confirms what's being said. In either case, the focus is on what the other person is saying, not on what you'd like to say next, or on what you'd like to hear.

"Management listens to us now." But that's not all they're saying. What they really mean is that management listens to what they say and does something about it. What they're saying is that real listening doesn't consist of just looking attentive and nodding your head occasionally... Employees must know that what they say will be heard and taken seriously, not dismissed out of hand. If they don't feel that, communication will dry up. [10]

It has always fascinated me that our education system is askew in how it teaches communication. We begin by learning how to read and write, but our speaking skills are generally left to take shape naturally. There is little training in how to listen effectively. This holds true for everything from high school to university courses and management training seminars.

■ **What courses are you and the members of your organization taking to improve listening skills?**

_____

_____

_____

_____

■ **How is this knowledge actually being used in daily conversations?**

_____

_____

_____

_____

■ What is your action plan for making effective listening a way of life in your organization?

_____

_____

_____

_____

■ Given what we have discussed in this section on communicating your organization's purpose, vision and focus, what are you going to do differently to communicate and implement your strategic plan?

_____

_____

_____

_____

Organizational soft-stuff staple 2: Arm the troops

Use the tools of training and development

There are six primary lessons to learn (in training and development).

1. Articulate a strategic vision...

2. Analyze strategic priorities and company needs (focus).

3. Distinguish between training and development...

4. Choose the right teachers and programs from inside and outside the organization.

5. Involve top managers at every stage of training and development–before, after and especially during the training and development process.

6. Evaluate training and development's educational value and cost effectiveness.[11]

The training and development marathon

A marathon race is 26 miles, 385 yards. The race of your professional life is about 45 years. The race of your personal life is about 75 years. To win those races, you must focus on the training you have to do before you cross the finish line.

Many of us spend over 16 years in educational institutions. Some of the skills we learn (in theory, at least) help lead us to our first jobs. We are promoted (again, in theory) based on our technical skill, experience and perhaps some communication ability. Yet when we become leaders, we sometimes find ourselves short of the skills we need.

> Our system of promotions tends to reward those who are successful at task accomplishment...But history has shown that the most productive leaders are those who have a balance of task orientation and group building and maintenance traits...traits that tend to strengthen the group as a group, fostering trust, mutual respect, harmony, dedication, and cohesiveness.[12]

Simply put, at a leadership level, the skills of planning, organizing, directing, controlling, rewarding and administering are no longer enough if you want to be successful.

To achieve results, you have to know three basic things

1. where you want to go,

2. how you're going to get there and

3. how you're going to inspire others to come with you.

The problem is, many leaders don't possess these skills. Hence, they fall into something I call "the leadership void."

The leadership void

The leadership void is the gap that exists between leaders and followers. It sends almost every newly promoted leader into an unsettled state of self-doubt and anxiety. One day, they are just "one of the boys [girls]." The next, they suddenly become one of "them."

Some corporations rely on three-to-four-week executive training programs to help new managers fill the void. That's tokenism, at best. For one thing, most of these programs still focus almost exclusively on the "hard" managerial skills of finance, accounting, production/operation techniques, marketing and human resources. With the possible exception of human resources, these skills are unfortunately of little value to managers unless they are also taught how the soft stuff relates to the hard stuff. How do you fill the void? I believe the answer lies in proper and continuous training and development.

"The black hole"

If you think education is expensive, try ignorance.

DEREK BOK
President, Harvard University

145

Some organizations spend vast sums of money on training and development. Yet this area is usually the first to be cut in times of economic hardship. This occurs because most organizations do not understand the importance of training and development in implementing a strategic plan. This key area is usually regarded as "discretionary," rather than "strategic."

Because I am a training consultant, some may think me self-serving in my opinion, but I believe training and development is anything but discretionary. I have found that organizations need to continually remind themselves why they are involved in it. It is not just a frill, and should not be a big black hole that simply eats money and produces no results.

Training and development is the vehicle you can use to implement the strategic plan. Without it, most organizational growth stops. Yes, you can reduce costs in the short term by reducing the amount of time and money committed to training and development, but in the long term, you may bleed the blood out of your organization.

To use an analogy: if purpose, vision and focus is your car, the soft stuff is both the fuel and the driver. Without driver training, the driver doesn't know how to get your car out of the garage. Even if he is lucky enough to get your car onto the street, he will very soon run the vehicle off the road. Whatever happens, other cars soon pass you by and you're left choking in their dust.

If cuts must be made in training and development, make them in the areas least important to your strategic plan. But *do not* cut training and development completely. If you do, you will drain the gas from your car and have no way of getting where you want to go–driver or no driver.

146

Training just because...

I am astounded with the reasoning of many people when I ask them why they select certain training programs. Their response is often a combination of: "It was time I went" (i.e., It's my turn now); "Because the program is there" (i.e., It's time I touched the ivy growing on the walls of higher learning); or "In my organization, to be promoted (fast-tracked) I have to take these development courses."

When I ask them if they've benefited from their courses, I am equally amazed. They usually just shrug their shoulders with a look of blank indifference. I think that's tragic–and a waste of time and money. The solution should be obvious:

- Participants should be told why the course is important to their jobs, careers, organization and customers.

- They should understand what they are expected to glean from the course.

- Follow-up should determine whether the objectives of the courses were met.

When I ask organizations how they pre-interview, discuss organization's and candidate's expectations or do a post analysis of programs attended, I often learn: nothing is required aside from a brief preliminary meeting, no discussions of expectations during or following the program, and for follow-up, there is the filing of a written report "grading" the program. This is discretionary programming and spending at its worst.

None of us can afford to waste time or money, especially in the economic climate of this decade. So, try answering a few of the following questions to see if your training and development is scoring you points or just sucking you into a black hole.

The man who was too old to learn was probably always too old to learn.

HENRY S. HASSKINS
American economist

■ **What training programs have you and the members of your organization attended in the past year?**

_____

_____

_____

_____

■ **How were the above specifically focused on your organization's purpose, vision and focus? (If you answer, "They weren't," or "I'm not sure," I'm sorry, but you just threw away time and money.)**

_____

_____

■ **Which programs might better focus on your organization's purpose, vision and focus?**

_____

_____

_____

- **Before you or members of your organization attend training programs, do you understand:**

  - Why you are being sent?

  - What your organization expects of you when you return?

  - Whether training and development is part of your organization's personal development appraisal system?

- **What have you done differently since returning from your last training program?**

_____

_____

_____

Organizational soft-stuff staple 3: Build bridges, not walls

Design working space that actually works

A corporation I know recently went through a merger. In the process, an initiative was undertaken to ensure office space was consistent between the two organizations. Enter the "space police." As you read this story, see if it reminds you of disputes you used to have with your siblings when you were a kid. Or, if you're a parent, perhaps it will remind you of mediations between your children about the size of their rooms. This is a corporate example, but it has parallels in many facets of life.

"Book 'em Danno"

After the merger, one manager was told his office was too large for his position in the company. He made several suggestions:

- Leave the office as is–he said he wouldn't tell anyone.

- Move the bookshelves and desks away from the wall to "shrink" his space to company specifications.

- Hang paper from the ceiling a distance from the wall so the size of the available floor space would conform to space regulations. He would write on the paper–"the space behind this paper doesn't exist. It is a figment of your imagination."

- Move out into the hallway and use the office for storage.

- Move others in with him.

- Find someone of a more senior level to move into his office–he would find other accommodation.

The space police were not amused–nor interested in any of his ideas. All they cared about was enforcing the rules. So, my friend and his staff had to find temporary space for over a month while the refurbishing crews moved in to make the space "right." By the time all the space inequities were addressed between the two organizations, the total cost was over $1 million.

You may be laughing, but my friend was crying. So should any leader worth their salt. As bizarre as this tale is, the scariest part is not the $1-million price tag. The scariest part is that this story is *true!*

Maybe you've experienced this kind of blatant inefficiency in your organization. If you haven't, you're lucky.

The kernel, as I see it, is this: we're on this earth to serve others, whether as parents, friends, brothers or sisters. In business, we serve the customer and support those who serve the customer. At home, we serve each other. We are not there simply to serve the organization.

Rules regarding space are usually developed to protect the status of those within an organization. Often, rules in general have little to do with meeting the organization's purpose, vision or focus. Worse still, they probably don't support those who are in a position to do just that. In fact, as was the case above, they can actually prevent a person from doing what needs to be done.

> *Most people want to make a contribution and be proud of what they do, but organizations typically teach us bad habits–to cut corners, protect our own turf, be political.[13]*
>
> ROBERT HAAS
> CEO, Levi Strauss

If our purpose, vision, focus or goal is to serve others–and that's what our goal should be if we intend to be viable in any organization (even something so seemingly non-customer-related as law enforcement, for example, has the motto "to serve and protect")–then we'd better focus on what's *really* important. Space, titles, position or perks don't matter a pinch to a customer. What matters is responsible service, high quality and the right price.

■ **Are there "space police" or others that serve similar roles in your organization?**

Circle one: **Yes**   **No**

■ If you answered yes, how are these individuals detracting from the purpose, vision and focus of your organization?

_____

_____

_____

■ How could you help them spend their time more effectively?

_____

_____

_____

■ What's the worst that can happen?

_____

_____

_____

■ What's the best that can happen?

_____

_____

_____

■ **What do you think will most likely happen?**

_____

_____

_____

How to design work space that works

Since 1987, BMW has emptied 10 office complexes of 6,000 engineers and support staff and relocated them to a $600-million Research and Engineering Center in Munich. The Center is laid out so that product engineers who design, say, the body structure of a car can sit across the hall from the factory engineers who design the machines that make the body. BMW found that engineers get 80% of their ideas from talking to each other, but only if their desks are within a 100-foot clear range.[14]

You may not have $600 million to invest in designing your work space, but BMW's level of financial commitment clearly supports the importance of a functional, communication-rich work place. This is also true of living space–especially at home. It may not cost you anything to improve communication within your environment. Chances are, however, that it will take you time and involve thought.

I once worked for a large bureaucratic organization. When I asked for line-of-sight communication with the people who worked with me, my request was denied. The "space police" said: "No one else's space is like that. Why should yours be any different?"

The result was an office box identical to everyone else's. There was no link with anyone except by telephone or computer. It was high-tech, but low-touch. It was also very ineffective. I wasted a lot of time trying to find my staff because I couldn't see through walls. Because of this inefficiency, the ultimate cost to the organization was far greater than what it would have been to create line-of-sight communication.

■ **Do you have line-of-sight and/or ample opportunity for informal communication with your key workers (or your manager)?**

Circle one: **Yes**   **No**

■ **If not, what's preventing line-of-sight and/or ample opportunity for informal communication?**

_____

_____

■ **How could you obtain such communication?**

_____

_____

Tearing down walls

More and more corporations are beginning to discover that to improve communication inside and outside an organization, they have to remove barriers.

Multi-national carpet and pigment manufacturer, Milliken Industries, of Spartanburg, South Carolina, has gone from "open door, to open office; to no office, no door." Managers have moved out onto the work floor with the people who report directly to them. Management–or more accurately what used to be management–is continuously asked the critical question: Who needs to be around whom to better serve the customer?

Now, communication at Milliken is immediate rather than by in and out baskets, memos, voice mail or even electronic mail. Lead times from order entry to customer delivery have been drastically cut. Customer concerns are handled on the spot, not through a customer complaint department.

Chaix & Johnson

Scott Kohno, a manager with the Los Angeles design firm, Chaix & Johnson, recently moved his office to the middle of the work floor. The result:

> *(S)taff contact is now 100 times more frequent. There are a million little discussions that move the company 10 times faster...It's the difference between being on the basketball floor instead of in the bleachers. You see the hysteria, the aggravation, the tension on faces, and you can appreciate it more...*[15]

Work around the system

Sometimes, improved communication isn't as simple as a move across the hall. One manager I know was promoted and moved to plushier offices on the "hallowed" 24th floor of his organization's building. He asked senior management if he could stay downstairs on the 10th floor with his people. The answer? An unequivocal "No!"

I asked him how he handled the situation. "I go in every morning, put my briefcase by my desk on the 24th floor and hang my jacket prominently on the back of my chair. I then head down to a small office I have managed to seconde on the 10th floor. All my calls are electronically forwarded there. If senior management comes around looking for me on the 24th floor, my secretary there calls me and I hotfoot it back up there.

"So far, no one has caught on. But it's only a matter of time before they find out what I'm doing and force me back upstairs."

◆ *What are you and your organization doing to break down physical barriers that impede communication?*

_____

_____

_____

_____

Organizational soft-stuff staple 4: Lead, follow or get out of the way

| Recognize the roles of a leader |

Over the years, much has been written about the roles of leaders. My goal here is not to duplicate those discussions, but to hone in on those skills that will help you succeed as a leader. They are by no means all the attributes that contribute to leadership excellence, but in my experience and research, they are the skills every good leader should not only know, but practise daily. They are:

- empower others
- "pancake" your pyramids
- communicate vision
- develop culture
- say thanks
- have the power of passion
- focus ferociously
- commit continuously
- serve and protect
- master our own destiny
- wear the mantle of leadership
- be honest, competent, visionary and inspirational

◆ Where leadership begins

The most significant thing we manage is behavior–our own, and those of others. I didn't say "dictate" or "manipulate." I said "manage." The better we understand our role as a manager/ leader, the more easily we'll obtain results from others. We hear a lot today about empowerment. But, although many managers are familiar with the term, some believe it is just a glorified method of delegation. It is not.

A middle manager I know was recently promoted to CEO. I asked him how his role as a leader changed. He wrote the following on a sheet of paper:

	Middle manager	CEO
Communicating vision	20%	50%
Empowering others	50%	20%
Developing culture	20%	20%
Saying thanks	10%	10%

The chart reveals at least part of the key to his promotion. As a middle manager, he spent most of his time empowering others. When I queried him on what he meant by empowerment, I discovered something else. He said he not only delegated jobs to others, he trusted them to do those jobs–completely. Once he'd assigned tasks, aside from periodic encouragement and "hands-off" updates, he let them run with their challenges.

Empowerment, he explained, is not just turning people loose to do what they want to do. Empowerment is providing individuals with the knowledge, skill (training and development), support (your role) and incentive (inspiration) to get the job done efficiently and effectively.

If you truly wish to empower someone, not just delegate, you must first assess that they have:

- the skills necessary to effectively complete the task

- the self-confidence and self-esteem required to handle the responsibility

A leader's role is to determine whether those they are leading possess the above qualities. If they do, those individuals have the potential to be empowered. To realize that potential, a leader must then add the catalyst–trust.

> In most companies, including ours (Levi Strauss), there is a gap between what the organization says it wants and what it feels like to work there. Those gaps between what you say and what you do erode trust in the enterprise and in the leadership, and they inhibit action. The more you can narrow the gap, the more people's energies can be released toward company purposes. [16]

Although behavior should be monitored, measurement should not be used as a hammer, but as a tool to assist those empowered in keeping on target. If we empower someone to do something, but then ask that they continually revisit us for approval, then they are not truly empowered because they are not truly trusted. Without trust, no empowerment can take place.

> *Don't tell people how to do things. Tell them what has to be done and they will amaze you with their ingenuity.*
>
> GEORGE PATTON
> General, U.S. Army

■ **Look over your daily calendar. How did you spend your time over the last month or so?**

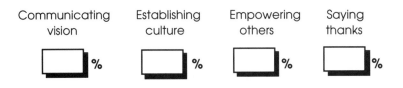

Communicating vision	Establishing culture	Empowering others	Saying thanks
____ %	____ %	____ %	____ %

■ **Specifically, how could you more effectively spend your time?**

_____

_____

_____

_____

_____

◆ "Pancake" your pyramids

In this era of flattening organizations, leadership styles have to change–from controlling to influencing, from participating to coaching, from bossing to teaching, from disciplining to

159

inspiring. In short, the traditional pyramid model of management/leadership in which decisions came from the top down has got to be flattened to the width of a pancake.

> *It's difficult to unlearn behaviors that made us successful in the past. Speaking rather than listening...Doing things on your own rather than collaborating. Making the decision yourself instead of asking different people for their perspectives. There's a whole range of behaviors that were highly functional in the old hierarchical organization that are dead wrong in the flatter, more responsive, empowered organization that we're seeking to become.* [17]

> ROBERT HAAS
> CEO, Levi Strauss

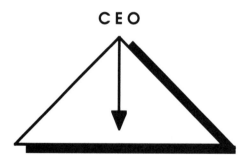

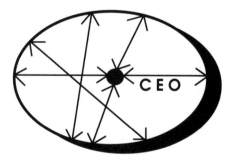

Although the subject of flattening organizations has been done to death, when most organizations today run into trouble, decision-making still reverts to "top-down."

I believe the opposite needs to occur. When you get into trouble sailing, for example, often the best solution is to let go of the sails and the rudder. The boat, miraculously, will turn into the wind and "right itself." The crew can then determine the best course to take to safety.

Next time you're in a tight spot, try turning the problem back over to your crew. It may be the quickest way to get the organization back to some degree of equilibrium until longer term solutions can be developed.

■ **Are you empowering others or are you just delegating?**

_____

■ **If you are not empowering others, why not? Do they (or you) lack the skills, the standards, the confidence or the self-esteem?**

_____

_____

■ **If they (or you) are lacking in the above areas how can you give them (or yourself) the opportunity to improve?**

_____

_____

_____

◆ Communicate vision

When my friend became a CEO, his challenge changed from empowering others to communicating vision. He met face to face with employees, customers, suppliers and shareholders to speak both informally and formally about that vision. Jan Carlzon, CEO of Scandinavian Airline Systems (SAS), did the same thing to turn that operation from a struggling airline into the industry's 1984 "Airline of the Year."

> *From my first day at SAS, I've made communicating, particularly with our employees, a top priority. In fact, during the first year I spent exactly half of my working hours out in the field talking to SAS people. The word going around was that any time three employees gathered, Jan Carlzon would probably show up and begin talking with them. It was my way of accepting responsibility and showing that my enthusiasm and involvement were genuine.* [18]

◆ Develop culture

With their focus on communication, both Carlzon and my friend began to shape their organizations' cultures. The two men learned to pay attention to the small victories because they were aware of them. Everyone's small efforts added up to large savings.

Corporate culture consists of the policies, beliefs, behaviors, atmosphere and physical environment of an organization. More often than not, culture is also a reflection of who is leading the organization. Banks are an interesting example. Walk into any branch of any bank and with a little careful observation, you can determine something of its culture simply by observing the staff's behavior. If they're

162

friendly and cooperative, chances are the branch manager is too. If they're officious and rules-oriented, look no further than their leader.

Leadership emulation is never more apparent than in branch organizations of this kind. Head office can have some impact, but the branch will take on the "cultural atmosphere" set to a large extent by the manager.

Dr. Walter Wright, president of Regent College, who sent the personal note that we discussed earlier in this Footprint, has developed a list of cultural values he wishes to instill in his organization. His list focuses on three areas: people, work and relationships. These are the touchstones of his organization's culture. (See chart on next page.)

The degree to which Regent College is able to achieve these cultural ideals is, of course, dependent on the behavior of the individuals who work and live there. It's like a country's constitution. What it contains is not what's most important. What's most important is how the individuals within that society (or organization) behave. The constitution of the former Soviet Union, for example, was written many years ago as reflecting one of the most liberated of all societies on Earth, yet only in the 1990s have serious attempts been made to transform the words of its constitution into action.

Regent College's list may seem idealistic to you, but Dr. Wright is quick to bring it down to earth.

I do not live these values consistently, and neither does Regent College–yet. But I am willing to be called to account for living in line with this list. And I expect to fail. I expect to be confronted by someone who cares. I expect to be forgiven and I expect to be empowered and encouraged to get up and take another step toward implementing our mission with a character shaped by these values.[19]

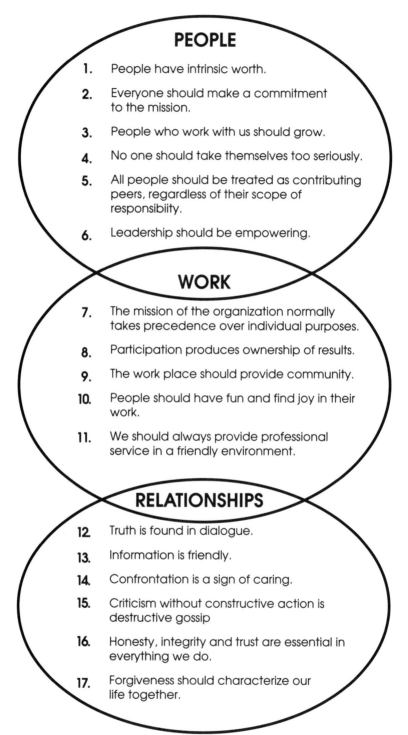

PEOPLE

1. People have intrinsic worth.

2. Everyone should make a commitment to the mission.

3. People who work with us should grow.

4. No one should take themselves too seriously.

5. All people should be treated as contributing peers, regardless of their scope of responsibiity.

6. Leadership should be empowering.

WORK

7. The mission of the organization normally takes precedence over individual purposes.

8. Participation produces ownership of results.

9. The work place should provide community.

10. People should have fun and find joy in their work.

11. We should always provide professional service in a friendly environment.

RELATIONSHIPS

12. Truth is found in dialogue.

13. Information is friendly.

14. Confrontation is a sign of caring.

15. Criticism without constructive action is destructive gossip

16. Honesty, integrity and trust are essential in everything we do.

17. Forgiveness should characterize our life together.

■ How would you describe the culture of your organization? For example, is it caring, trusting, positive or is it destructive, political, negative?

_____

_____

_____

_____

■ What parts of your organization's culture do you like? Dislike?

_____

_____

_____

_____

_____

■ What are the sources of your particular culture? How could your organization's culture be improved?

_____

_____

_____

_____

165

■ **How could you begin to change the culture, if necessary?**

_____

_____

_____

_____

◆ Say thanks

Although this category has the smallest amount of time allocated to it in the chart described earlier, it is perhaps the most significant. The success of all the other categories depends on this one.

Saying thanks doesn't always have to be done with money. In fact, it's often better if money isn't used at all. Verbal acknowledgments go a long way. You cannot readily predict someone else's behavior when they are verbally or physically punished. However, you can usually predict the result of positive reinforcement: It's usually positive behavior.

■ **How often do you say thanks for work well done?**

_____

■ **How do you currently acknowledge positive behavior?**

_____

_____

■ **Do you say thanks enough?**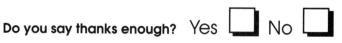

■ **Who are some people you should thank in the next 24 hours?**

_____

_____

_____

◆ **Have the power of passion**

Besides empowering others, communicating vision, developing culture and saying thanks, successful leaders possess another element of excellence. It is passion. In business, it can be passion for the products and services an organization produces. In family life, it can be pride in family members. But regardless of the venue, hardly a breath is spoken or an activity undertaken by a passionate leader in which they are not in some way spreading the "gospel" of their belief in themselves, and in their organization.

Passion is more than a strong determination and belief in something. It is a burning desire, an almost possessed drive that keeps individuals moving in spite of the obstacles. It is the fire in the belly and in the eye of the tiger. To succeed, you have to have it.

Passion emanates from an individual's values–their core beliefs. Someone with passion operates from the essence of themselves. They know who they are and they do what they love. They are true to themselves.

Unlike so many leadership skills, passion cannot be learned–but over time, you can acquire it. It is important in leading others because if a leader does not have it, she or he cannot hope to create it in others. Hence, others will be easily frustrated and stopped by obstacles.

■ **What really excites you emotionally and intellectually? What would you do for absolutely nothing? What would get you out of bed in the morning yearning to get started?**

_____

_____

_____

Discussion:

If your list above does not include what you presently do most of the day, you might want to re-evaluate your life. You may not be realizing your potential. Nor are you likely to bring it out in others. No true leader lives dispassionately.

◆ Focus ferociously

Another important role of a first-class leader is focus. They know what has to be done and they set about doing it. Because they are focused, their followers are focused as well.

David Kearns, former CEO of Xerox, says:

> _To effect a cultural change, I realized, you need to zero in on the customer above all else. So I feel it was an error to have had all three objectives equal (improving return on assets, increasing market share, bettering customer satisfaction)...I really believe you have to train your attention on the ultimate user of the products and that will get the hard financial results. Had I done...(this) from the start, I feel we might have shaved at least a year and maybe two from this whole (change) process._[20]

168

Focus is not restricted to the tasks to be done that day, that week or that month. It is an understanding that to perpetuate excellence, we must also focus on what is excellent around us–in others, in our environment and in our world.

■ **What are your three areas of greatest focus at present?**

1. _____

2. _____

3. _____

■ **What does your organization's purpose, vision, focus and strategic plan say your three areas of focus should be?**

1. _____

2. _____

3. _____

■ **Where are the areas of inconsistency, if any?**

_____

_____

_____

■ **How could you change this situation, if necessary?**

_____

_____

_____

◆ Commit continuously

As I said at the beginning of this Footprint, too many organizations, like individuals, want to get to "the bottom line" immediately after the purpose, vision and focus steps. In this world of quick fixes and instant answers, they want instant results. There are no results, especially instant results, without commitment.

A manager I know admitted to me once that he had started several strategic planning initiatives, but all had fallen short because of his lack of commitment. He explained his painful learning process by drawing this diagram:

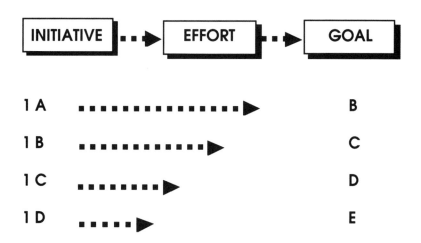

The manager explained, " I would start an initiative '1' with the objective to accomplish each of goals 'B, C, D, E' in about four weeks. My problem was that I kept running out of gas after about three weeks. Over time, my staff began to realize this. So, rather than jumping on the new initiative bandwagon with me, they learned to put out only enough effort to appear to be supporting me. In actual fact, they were simply waiting me out until I ran out of steam and went back to 'business as usual.'

170

"I've since learned that I've got to stay with it. I can't expect instant results. Nor can I delegate key initiatives to others and forget about them. They're my babies. If I stop championing them, they die.

"Now, before starting a new initiative, I carefully consider whether or not I'm truly committed to carrying it out. Consequently, my action flow chart now looks more like..."

And he proceeded to draw this diagram:

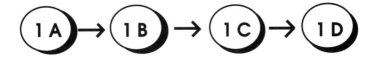

My friend was not alone in his plight:

Some of the managers were lamenting about how the company was being run as if it were a Baskin-Robbins inventing its flavour of the month. One month the key word was growth. Another month it was cost-control. Another it was quality. Nothing seemed to stick... [21]

DAVID KEARNS
Former CEO, Xerox

The process of continuous improvement through the soft stuff never ends because it's just that–continuous. Fortunately, organizations are gradually waking up to this fact. They are learning that bottom-line-driven leaders may only accomplish a short-term quick fix. Long-term commitment and staying power is what's most important.

Your attitude at the beginning of a task largely determines your attitude at the end of a task.

KEN ALLEN
Men's gymnastics coach,
University of Wisconsin

THE PAST

■ **What were some of your past leadership initiatives?**

_____

_____

_____

■ **How long were they in place?**

_____

_____

_____

■ **What were the results of your initiatives?**

_____

_____

_____

THE PRESENT

- **What are some of your present leadership initiatives?**

1. _____

2. _____

3. _____

- **On a scale of 1 to 10 (10 being the highest), how would you rate your level of commitment to each of these initiatives?**

1.   1   2   3   4   5   6   7   8   9   10

2.   1   2   3   4   5   6   7   8   9   10

3.   1   2   3   4   5   6   7   8   9   10

- **When do you expect to achieve results?**

1. _____

2. _____

3. _____

- **Can you hang on that long?**

1. YES ☐   NO ☐

2. YES ☐   NO ☐

3. YES ☐   NO ☐

Discussion:

If your commitment is wavering, see if you can re-acquaint yourself with why you began your initiative in the first place. If you can no longer remember, or your reasons are vague, chances are the initiative did not have the proper purpose, vision or focus. If it did, it may help your level of commitment to return to that purpose, vision or focus.

◆ To serve and protect

Good leaders must know how and when to protect those they lead from the organization. That's right, they must know how to protect those they lead *from* the organization.

In almost every organization, some individuals are intent on getting in the way of progress. Some do it consciously to defend their territory or preserve the status quo. Others are completely unaware that they are doing it at all. Therefore, one of the key roles of a leader is to fight for the rights of those they lead so they can get on with their jobs.

> *The belief that it is possible for individuals to have the feeling that they are creating an organization of their own choosing is radical...People at the top have tremendous impact, yet we are constantly reminded that in very practical ways, the inmates run the prison.* [22]
>
> PETER BLOCK
> Author, consultant

◆ Mastering our own destiny

Even small events initiated by leaders can create the kind of protective atmosphere necessary for change. An upper-level

174

manager with a major oil and gas firm was recently transferred to a new division. To make communication with his employees easier, he began looking for a round meeting table for his office. He called those in charge of supplying furniture and asked for one. He didn't like what he found–"The Furniture Police."

The furniture police told him there were no round tables available and that he would have to put in a capital requisition for one. This process could take a year or more and there would be no guarantee he would actually get a table. Times were tough and even though round tables cost the same as square ones, round tables were not standard company issue.

In desperation, the manager drove to a furniture store nearby, bought a round table, loaded it into the trunk of his car and hauled it up to his office. He dragged the square table into the hallway and instructed the furniture police to pick it up. He put the round table on his expense account and submitted it for reimbursement. It got through.

The message in this manager's actions rang clear to his employees: Things were changing and he was helping lead the way. By refusing to conform to the organization's rules, he was indirectly protecting his employees from those rules as well. They realized he would back them in their own efforts to become more effective.

Just as one of the roles of a leader is to protect the troops from the organization, a leader must similarly protect the organization's customers and suppliers. We'll talk more about that later in this Footprint when we discuss the importance of simplicity.

The moral of the furniture story is simple: Do what you need to do to get the job done. Damn the torpedoes. To heck with policies that limit and constrain human initiative. If it will make your job easier, improve your organization's bottom line, or service the customer better, do it. But remember– the key to making successful changes is know you can always

175

justify your actions. That way, if someone questions your move, they'll eventually learn to leave you alone. This is something I have learned from others as well as from my own personal experience.

Today's marketplace is competitive. You need to be someone worth keeping, not someone discarded because you've been forgotten. Maintaining the status quo may be more dangerous in the long run than trying to make short-term improvements–for you and for your organization. Why? Because you just fade into the woodwork–you become part of the furniture. Furniture eventually gets replaced–sometimes by new, more useful furniture. My advice to leaders: If you have to go down, go down with both guns blazing. It's a helluva lot better than getting gunned down on the sidelines without ever having fired a shot.[23]

■ **What are some archaic and apparently counter-productive systems entrenched in your organization? (You may need more than the space provided)**

_____

_____

_____

_____

_____

■ **How have these systems limited your effectiveness?**

_____

_____

_____

_____

_____

■ **How could you work around these systems to the benefit of yourself, others and your organization?**

_____

_____

_____

_____

_____

■ **What could be some of the negative outcomes of your actions?**

_____

_____

_____

_____

_____

■ **How could you justify your actions?**

_____

_____

_____

_____

_____

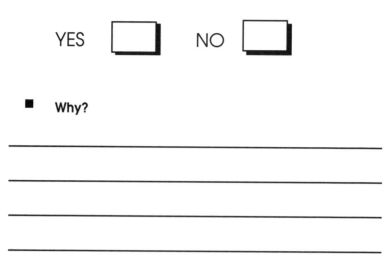

- **Are you prepared to take the necessary risks to encourage change?**

YES ☐   NO ☐

- **Why?**

_____

_____

_____

_____

◆ Wearing the mantle of leadership

Another important leadership role is knowing how to nurture respect. Good leaders know they carry a "mantle" of leadership– a host of expectations from those they lead.   Some expectations are realistic; others are not.

Americans expect their president to act in a manner consistent with the office. The queen of England carries the same responsibility.

This is precisely why some organizations do not promote from within a branch. They recognize that it is difficult to lead those who were once your peers. In some corporations, you once shared a common "enemy"–the person whose position you could now hold. These organizations often promote people by moving them away from the branch, sometimes to a new city.

◆ Be honest, competent, visionary and inspirational

You cannot manage men into battle.
You manage things, you lead people.

GRACE MURRAY HOPPER
Admiral, U.S. Navy

A leading management publication lists the top four attributes followers look for in their leaders (in order of importance):

1. honesty
2. competency
3. visionary
4. inspirational [24]

Honesty conveys trust, believability and integrity–the ability of leaders to follow through with what they say they will do. (Without this one, all others are impossible to fulfil.)

I hope I shall possess firmness and virtue enough to maintain what I consider the most enviable of titles–the character of an honest man.

GEORGE WASHINGTON
First president
of the United States

Competency in a leader means having the abilities and skills to lead.

The leader must know, must know he knows, and must make it abundantly clear to those around him that he knows.

CLARENCE B. RANDALL
Former chairman,
Inland Steel Corporation

179

"Visionary" describes leaders who develop and clearly communicate a destination.

> *Momentum comes from a clear vision of what the corporation ought to be, from a well-thought-out strategy to achieve that vision, and from carefully conceived and communicated directions and plans which enable everyone to participate and be publicly accountable in achieving those plans.*[25]
>
> MAX DEPREE
> Chairman,
> Herman Miller Group

Inspiration in a leader means encouraging others to take part in the journey by praising them.

> *I have yet to find the man, however exalted his station, who did not do better work and put forth greater effort under a spirit of approval than under a spirit of criticism.*
>
> CHARLES SCHWAB
> American industrialist

■ **Realistically, how many of these leadership attributes do you possess?**

Circle the ones you possess:

1   2   3   4

■   Complete the following table. Beside each, rate
yourself from 1 to 10. Beside that, briefly describe
how you plan to increase or maintain your score.

HONESTY

1   2   3   4   5   6   7   8   9   10

Action to increase or maintain score:

_____

_____

_____

COMPETENCY

1   2   3   4   5   6   7   8   9   10

Action to increase or maintain score:

_____

_____

_____

VISIONARY

1   2   3   4   5   6   7   8   9   10

Action to increase or maintain score:

_____

_____

_____

INSPIRATIONAL

1   2   3   4   5   6   7   8   9   10

Action to increase or maintain score:

_____

_____

_____

Discussion:

If you score eight or above in some of these areas, congratulations! Your purpose, vision and focus should help you maintain these attributes. If your scores are less than eight, your purpose, vision, focus and soft stuff should help you establish the guidelines necessary to attain higher scores for these attributes.

Organizational soft-stuff staple 5: The right ruler

| Measure creatively and meaningfully |

Most leaders believe they manage people. You may agree. While it's true, it doesn't tell the whole story. The whole story is really that effective leaders manage behavior, not people. If you want to change the results of your organization and produce continuous improvement, you don't change your people (although for many organizations that is a frequently used alternative). You change their behavior.

> *While most (job) positions are associated with tasks to be accomplished, a behavior-accomplishment distinction always is possible. We assert that the single most important thing that managers can do to increase employee productivity is to engage in this distinction. Managers and employees together should be able to precisely specify those activities needed by each person to fulfil their respective obligations to the company. Equipped with this information, managers would be taking the first step toward managing behavior, not people.* [26]

Measure creatively

To determine if something is being continuously improved through changed behavior, we need a method of measuring that behavior. This is where creative measurement is useful.

In this section, we'll talk first about the foundation on which creative measurement is built. Then we'll discuss a few examples.

Playing the scoreless game

One company with which I work said they were doing everything well. Yet they were not measuring their progress towards their goals. This is like playing a game and not keeping score. The surprise comes at match point when you suddenly discover you're in danger of elimination. That's why creative measurement is so important. It allows you to monitor your progress before month's end, quarterly end, year-end or *the end.*

> *When employees got the tools plus a management that would listen to them, they immediately grabbed the opportunity to improve quality. After all, they had been telling management for 10 or 20 years that things were all screwed up and nobody ever listened to them. Now, they finally had some techniques they could use to identify, document, and prove beyond a shadow of a doubt that things were in fact screwed up.* 27

Creative measurement and continuous improvement are inseparably linked. In business, creative measurement should be linked directly or indirectly to customer service.

In manufacturing, faster production can mean the customer's needs are met faster. On-time delivery means they won't be kept waiting and lower production costs can mean lower prices. Higher quality means the customer doesn't have to get the product serviced as often, or even at all.

Nothing is particularly hard if you divide it into small jobs.

HENRY FORD
American automobile
manufacturer

The heart of the measurement matter

The three keys to creative measurement are:

1. establish the results you wish

2. between you and the members of your organization, determine the measures necessary to achieve those results

3. determine the specific behaviors necessary to achieve those measures

Thus:

BEHAVIOR ▪ ▪ ▪▶ MEASUREMENT ▪ ▪ ▪▶ RESULT

The power of creative measurement is that those working must see a direct link between themselves and, through their work, others. The key to measuring creatively is to break down each job into its smallest components. For a machinist spinning a piece of metal on a lathe, it may be the number of sweeps he or she makes across the metal. Or, it might be the

185

number of pieces they create without a defect. This works equally well in sales, trucking, administration, even oil well operations–as we'll see.

Creative measurement in sales

I once worked with a distributor of high-tech equipment. The company wanted to increase its sales in a highly competitive market. Two options were considered:

> **1.** hire more sales people or
>
> **2.** improve the effectiveness of the current sales force

With further thought, company officials realized the organization was actually quite effective in getting prospective customers into their showrooms for demonstrations. And, their salespeople succeeded in closing roughly half of those customers.

Company officials determined if they increased the closing ratio of their sales force from 50 to 60 per cent, they would increase sales by $1.2 million–about a 5 per cent increase in overall sales. They, therefore, developed the following behavioral map to achieve their $1.2 million sales increase goal:

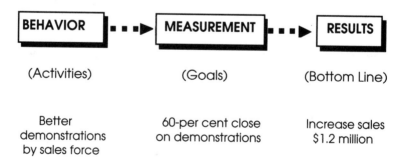

BEHAVIOR ▪ ▪ ▪▶	MEASUREMENT ▪ ▪ ▪▶	RESULTS
(Activities)	(Goals)	(Bottom Line)
Better demonstrations by sales force	60-per cent close on demonstrations	Increase sales $1.2 million

The behavior of the organization's salesforce then shifted from increasing sales (bottom line) to focusing on the specific activities (above the bottom line) that would deliver success. Management also made a shift. It began concentrating on what was required to present better demonstrations (the soft stuff). Customer questionnaires were developed to determine which elements of the demonstrations were most effective. This information was then shared with the salesforce so they could change their behavior. The salesforce was also given additional training with a greater emphasis on closing the sale.

If we take the above example as a model, we can develop a simple but powerful system for improving results through creative measurement:

- Begin by determining the bottom-line results you want.
- Decide which measures can help you achieve those results.
- Determine the specific behaviors that will enable you to make that measurement.
- Decide how to improve the behavior.

One of the beauties of creative measurement is that it can help you pinpoint problems quickly and easily. If sales start to decline, for example, a quick check of your behavior modification system may determine if the problem is related to your salesforce. It may not be. Outside influences such as economic conditions, price point, competition and the quality and utility of the product may also play a major role. Whatever the case, creative measurement could give you some idea where the problem lies. Pinpointing the source of the problem is half of solving it.

187

Learning about leadership by taking risks

Leadership, like swimming, cannot be learned by reading about it.

HENRY MINTZBERG
Canadian educator and
management writer

There are dozens of other examples of the importance of creative measurement. I would like to share four with you, and thereby highlight some of the ways a measuring stick can detract from or contribute to your success as a leader. The real test of your mettle will come from your ability to learn from these examples and, through your own creativity, develop measurement methods for individuals (including yourself) in your own organization.

Accidental results— creative measurement in trucking

A manager I know was recently promoted to head of a field operation in the oil industry. His mission was to decrease costs and increase revenue. Many managers had preceded him. All had failed.

In the year before his appointment, there were 35 accidents involving company vehicles. At an estimated $20,000 cost per accident in repairs and downtime, about $700,000 had been lost.

Management believed the accidents could be divided into two categories: no-fault and avoidable.

188

Here is how the man carried out his mission:

♦ **Year one**

Within a few weeks, the manager met with the drivers and told them what each accident cost the company. He went on to explain that he would dismiss anyone who caused an "avoidable" accident.

♦ **Year one results**

By the end of the first year, accidents had increased from 35 to 39. Several were determined to have been avoidable and as a consequence, some people were dismissed.

The manager's assessment was succinct: "I certainly didn't decrease the number of accidents. What I did do was lose some good people. I also increased the creativity of my drivers in writing up accident reports."

On one report, the manager noted, a deer attacked a truck. In another, a telephone pole suddenly moved into the middle of the road. In yet another, a pole moved into the side of a truck while the driver was sitting in a restaurant.

The manager's conclusion was clear: "Communicating 'corporate concerns' and disciplining with punitive measures didn't work."

♦ **Year two**

The next year, my friend got smarter. He met with the drivers, divided them into teams of four and told them the goal for the year was zero accidents. He told them for every three months a team was accident-free, he would buy them lunch.

Daily accident-free periods for all groups were recorded and posted in each team location.

♦ **Year two results**

The results were remarkable. There were only three accidents all year. His conclusion: "We had a lot of fun. We determined that the main cause of the accidents was people driving too fast. In a couple of cases, the groups met to tell a fellow member to slow down. In one case, they asked that one member be "retired" from the group.

"The lesson for me was simple: **Set standards from the employees' point of view, not from your own.** Set measurement standards that are a challenge, but simple to follow. Make the measurement periods short enough so successes can be recognized quickly. You can travel a long way with short steps when you know where you're going and that the goal is worthwhile and attainable for the people involved."

The gas game—
creative measurement in the oil industry

This same manager was entrusted with reducing propane consumption on an oil well site. The propane was used to heat thick, heavy oil coming out of the ground into a thinner liquid that could be poured into tanker trucks for transportation from the well site. Potential annual savings were estimated in the hundreds of thousands of dollars.

◆ **Year one**
The manager advised the operating crews of the problem and the annual cost. Then, he asked them for suggestions to resolve the problem. Some suggestions were put forward.

◆ **Results of year one**
Although some improvements were made, there was no significant reduction in propane consumption.

◆ **Year two**
Propane was delivered by truck to storage facilities on each of the well sites. A ticket indicating the amount of fuel delivered was produced each time. The manager decided to count the number of tickets produced at each site. The number of deliveries was recorded and posted at each site, and

190

the previous years' numbers were also posted as a bench mark for comparison. Naturally, the fewer the tickets, the less propane consumed.

"It was really quite amazing," the manager observed. "Employees began having meetings on how they could reduce propane deliveries. They found they could reduce propane consumption by turning the heaters on only a day or so before the tanker trucks took delivery of the crude. They had been leaving them on all the time. Some of them found ingenious ways of actually taking the gas coming off the well itself and using that gas to heat the tanks. Needless to say, the savings were substantial.

"I learned that you should explain the issue in the employees' language. Keep the measurement system simple. Publish the measures so everyone can see them. Then, give the employees total freedom to determine how they can improve."

Measuring the unmeasurable– creative measurement in administration

Creative measurement can be used in almost any situation– from propane consumption to personal interaction. It can even be used to improve something as apparently unmeasurable as trust.

In a large organization, a manager noticed people did not trust the administration. So, he set an annual goal of 50 "trust commitments" from his administrative personnel. A trust commitment was any personal interaction (no matter how small) that led to better relations between administrative and other employees. Examples included everything from a commitment to cooperate more closely on contracts with tight time lines to creating faster turnaround on accounts payable and receivable. Employees were asked to come up with ideas to achieve higher levels of trust.

191

The immediate result was more face-to-face meetings, business lunches and get-togethers after work. The conclusion was that to increase trust, employees needed to increase personal (not paper) contacts and keep track of commitments made during these contacts. In light of the examples cited earlier in this Footprint, consider the following flow chart:

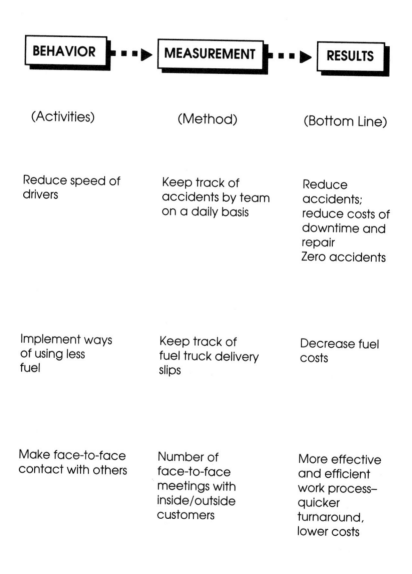

BEHAVIOR	MEASUREMENT	RESULTS
(Activities)	(Method)	(Bottom Line)
Reduce speed of drivers	Keep track of accidents by team on a daily basis	Reduce accidents; reduce costs of downtime and repair Zero accidents
Implement ways of using less fuel	Keep track of fuel truck delivery slips	Decrease fuel costs
Make face-to-face contact with others	Number of face-to-face meetings with inside/outside customers	More effective and efficient work process– quicker turnaround, lower costs

You'll never know until you ask– creative measurement in banking

A bank set out to change the way its tellers handled customers. It established daily objectives called "blast targets" and measured how often tellers asked customers about branch marketing initiatives such as credit cards, retirement savings plans and mortgages. Tellers were teamed with trained sales staff who followed up when the customer expressed an interest in discussing the services further.

The branches whose tellers asked the greatest number of questions very quickly surpassed the sales of branches whose tellers asked fewer questions.

■ Pick one area in which you'd like to increase your effectiveness. What are the results you need?

_____

_____

_____

■ What is one creative measurement goal you can set that will enable you to achieve the results you want–in your followers' language?

_____

_____

_____

_____

193

Behavior of outstanding performers	Measurement method in employee terms	Results in your terms

Carl Sewell and Paul B. Brown in their book *Customers for Life* sum up the six keys to creative measurement:

- Will the employees relate to the indicator?

- Are the indicators available at least every two weeks? (Some suggest a minimum of every week.)

- If the score takes any more than 15 minutes per day to track, it's probably not feasible to do it...

- The most effective measures are simply stated. Putting things in terms of units is best, dollars are second best, third best would be percentages. *Ironically, management usually relates to things in exactly the reverse order–percentages, then dollars and, finally, units. (my emphasis)*

- Instead of scrap, report yield. Don't measure late deliveries. Track on-time shipments. People would much rather shoot for a goal than avoid making a mistake. [28]

- Post the results and share the information. People are naturally competitive, want to do a good job, and like to know how they're doing. [29, 30]

194

Organizational soft-stuff staple 6: Keep it simple, stupid

| Can the complexity |

I once did strategic planning for a major ski resort in the Canadian Rockies. To reduce loss of revenue, management had a policy at the ticket window. Those who sold lift tickets were not authorized to give refunds once the ticket (which cost $35) was purchased. Authorization for refunds had to come from the vice-president.

When a customer requested a refund, everyone at the resort tried to find the vice-president of marketing. If he could be found, he would ski down the hill and determine if a refund was in order. This typically took 30 minutes or more.

When I queried the vice-president about this policy, he explained that part of his role was to protect the organization from customers who were trying to "take advantage" of the system.

I swallowed hard. In subsequent discussions with the group at this resort, we helped change the policy by assessing the value of a repeat customer. A lifetime customer was estimated at 15 years. Assuming she or he spent $500 a year on a season's pass and an additional $10 per 30 annual visits on food and other items, the lifetime financial value of one customer was $12,000.

Later, I heard about six skiers who five years earlier asked for their money back one very cold day. They were refused not on the merit of their request, but because the vice-president was busy with other business and was unable to get down to see them.

They'd never been back.

195

The ski hill's policy saved the resort $210 that day. But it cost them far more in the long run–thousands of dollars in repeat business and goodwill. A happy customer tells three to six people, but an unhappy one tells at least ten.

What's the solution? It's obvious, of course. Show the ticket agents how to handle refunds quickly and amicably and empower them to make those decisions. Get the names and addresses of all those who receive refunds. Have the vice-president or CEO contact them by phone or letter expressing their concern. Send them a gift coupon for the restaurant or gift shop on the hill. It's a lot easier to keep customers than to go out and find new ones. It's also a lot cheaper.

Giving the customer the gas

An "elite" European automobile agency with whom I've had the displeasure of doing business used to provide loaner vehicles to customers who convinced the dealer they deserved one for the day. The cars came with empty gas tanks. Why? Since the agency provided a loaner, it believed it should not also pay for the gas. This "empty tank" policy was initiated because some customers returned vehicles with less gas in them than when they had gone out.

As a result, customers sometimes drove unsuspectingly off the lot only to run out of gas two or three blocks from the dealership!

I have shared this story many times in my seminars. Without fail, participants are astonished that an organization could be so blatantly insensitive towards their customers.

Again, the solution is obvious–fill the cars with gas and, if you have to, tell the customers they will be charged for the fuel they haven't replaced when they return.

But that's not the point.

196

To protect and not to serve

The point is most organizational rules (internal space and furniture rules included) are designed to protect the organization, not service the customer. Anyone who thinks they'll stay in business by protecting the organization is wrong. They may last a year or two, but they won't last 10 years and they sure won't last 100.

I call this method of operating "bunker behavior." By protecting itself in the trenches, an organization may appear to be safe in the short-term, but it won't go anywhere in the long run. Worse still, it's slowly starving to death because it's cutting off its financial supply line–its customers.

What this all comes down to is simplicity. The new way of doing business is to find ways to make it easier and simpler to do business–for you, your organization and especially, for your customers.

■ **Assume you have just been made president of your organization. How could you better serve the customer and simplify your policies at the same time?**

_____

_____

_____

_____

_____

_____

■ **If you were a customer, how could your organization better serve you?**

_____

_____

_____

_____

_____

_____

In summary, keep your primary goal in mind. You must simplify your procedures so you can directly serve your customers–whether that "customer" is your employee, your supplier or your end customer. Cut out any rules that don't directly serve them.

Organizational soft-stuff staple 7: Passion, power and pizazz

Inspire Others

People like to be inspired. They like the sizzle of being part of an exciting event. They enjoy living in a city with championship teams, world-class ballet or stirring opera. They like chilling mystery theatre, roaring good comedy and great live music. Our fondest memories are filled with times of greatness.

The city of Calgary still hasn't gotten over the euphoric buzz of hosting the 1988 Olympic Winter Games. It ignited a passion and singleness of purpose like nothing since the oil boom of the late 1940s and the 1970s. For 16 days, the world's eye focused on Calgary. More importantly, for that fast and furious period, Calgarians had a common goal, a shared dream. It was fantastic. City residents may not remember who won which event, but they all recall the excitement of being part of the Olympic experience. Most of the people involved in the Games–more than 10,000 of them–weren't paid a dime. They were volunteers.

We need victories to produce sizzle in our lives. Great leaders know the value in celebrating small successes on the way to big achievements. Moment-by-moment, positive experiences that are shared and recognized are the stuff of great journeys. In fact, they help ensure a triumphant finish–even if the finish line is redefined during the approach.

Celebrating through the struggle

The important thing to recognize is that it takes a team, and the team ought to get credit for the wins and the losses. Successes have many fathers, failures have none.

> PHILIP CALDWELL
> Chairman,
> Ford Motor Company

As I write this book, industries throughout North America are foundering. Revenues are down and costs are up. The oil and gas, airline, computer and automotive industries are laying employees off by the tens of thousands. Almost everyone is hurting. "Cost containment" is the rallying cry. It's depressing.

199

What disappoints me is I know there are small achievements occurring in these organizations every day, yet no one appears to be celebrating them. Few are even acknowledged.

Even if your organization's team is behind 50 to nothing and you score one point, it should be celebrated—by all team members. Everyone should congratulate the individual who scored the point. We'd celebrate if we were ahead 50 to nothing, so why change when we are behind?

There is magic in emphasizing the positive, even in difficult circumstances. It's easy to focus on the trials of a difficult trail ahead and miss the flowers beside it.

How to celebrate . . . and how not to

One day, a government administrator I know was taken to lunch by his superiors. They commended him highly for increasing employee morale, achieving cost reductions and speeding up work in a department known for its shoddy and slow performance. Then they presented him with an "under the table" cheque in recognition for his efforts. Since this was not normal procedure, they told him to tell no one about receiving it.

I asked him how he felt about receiving the money. He replied with one word: "Devastated." Although he was pleased with the size of the cheque, he was disappointed his recognition was totally private. Neither his peers nor his employees knew of it.

Recognition is the magic elixir that motivates individuals to behave in ways that produce positive results. All of us want praise. Few of us receive it. As a society, we criticize more than we reward. "But that's their job!" we so often say. "Why do we have to recognize anyone for doing their job?"

Through recognition, you ensure that the individual's behavior continues. Others also realize what is significant.

Employees of the moment

I am dead set against "Employee of the Month" programs. I am equally against "Employees of the Year." I much prefer "Employees of the Moment."

I have seen numerous organizations, particularly hotels and restaurants, display photos of their "Employees of the Month." In one hotel, I asked the manager why the employee received the award. He didn't know. I suspect this is the case in most organizations and this is what concerns me. I picture managers running around every month trying to find a reason to honor an employee. The same must occur at year-end.

For recognition to be effective, it must occur right after the achievement and it's best while the person is still sweating from the exertion. Thirty days or three hundred and sixty-five days later is too late.

The reason for the recognition must also be made clear. A simple photo isn't sufficient, nor is a gold watch, a pin or a trip to Hawaii. Explain to other employees or to the public why the individual is being honored. Along with their picture, display an explanation.

If possible, publish an announcement in the newspaper. People love to see their names in print. They cut it out, frame it and put it on their wall. They keep it in a scrapbook for their grandchildren. The more public you can make the recognition, the more powerful it will become.

Motivational meetings

Just as individuals need to be recognized, so do groups. I recommend managers put aside at least half a day every month for recognizing the efforts of their team. Some organizations allocate two days a month–and they're mandatory.

Use this time to collectively determine:

- where your team has been in the past month,

- where you are now, and

- where you want to go in the month ahead.

Measuring your success

To achieve your objectives for the month ahead, measure everything you can. These measures, based on your organization's purpose, vision and focus, must be an integral part of the monthly review process. Where there are victories, celebrate; where there are difficulties, determine how to rectify the situation.

Monthly measurement reviews allow you to pull away from everyday distractions and recharge your batteries so you can more effectively handle daily pressures.

Report for month of

■ **What areas are we measuring?**

_____

_____

■ **What areas are on target and require celebration?**

_____

_____

■ **What areas are behind expectations and what action is required?**

_____

_____

_____

The inspiration/information mix

One manager I know organizes meetings so they are 25 per cent inspiration and 75 per cent information. Videos, speakers, skits, awards, articles or books all play a part. His meetings are so well received that everyone wants to get in on the act. Spontaneity is common in the way employees report, congratulate each other and solve problems.

Some reports are dry and factual. Others are presented using water pistols and other props, from balloons to novelties of all kinds. Skits, in particular, can be effective in loosening up organizations that have become encrusted in tradition. Videotape them if you can. One planning meeting I observed is now a training video for new employees. Part of inspiration is getting people to loosen up so their creative juices flow. Meetings don't have to be gloomy, serious or boring.

Achievements can be recognized by leaders in equally wonderful ways. In one case I know of, a manager asked the human resources department to assist him in buying achievement plaques. Their response was typical: "If we make this available to you, everyone will want it. Where will it stop?"

203

Instead of plaques, he used his desktop publishing system to print some award certificates. Naysayers said: "No one's going to get off on those cheap certificates. You'll embarrass yourself."

His creativity and individual attention brought cheers from his staff. The next morning, the employees posted their certificates on their office doors–even though this practice was against company policy. The certificates became a regular part of his meetings. All were highly coveted.

A cautionary note here. Not everyone should *have* to receive an award. Attempts should be made to ensure that up to 70 per cent receive individual recognition. If everyone knows they are in line for some form of recognition, it cheapens the achievement for those who actually make targets. However, ensure that everyone shares in the celebration of group achievements.

The message is in the ritual

Every year at the University of Calgary, graduation exercises are held for participants in the Executive Development Program. Prior to the ceremony, participants usually ask: "Why are we doing this? Can't you just mail us our certificate?" Undaunted, we proceed. In full gowns, participants parade nervously across the stage to receive their "diplomas." The event takes place before peers and sometimes, family members.

I know of organizations that take great care in orchestrating their celebrations of achievement. IBM has a 100% Sales Club for its leading sales people–a prestigious and elite group. Milliken Industries of South Carolina uses "sharing meetings" or "rallies" where accomplishments are shared openly among staff members. The celebration is done with sizzle and creativity. Senior management attends and applauds the successes.

204

Rituals like these celebrate milestones employees have achieved. Organizations, and more importantly, leaders, must recognize these accomplishments in more than humdrum ways. It goes beyond business. It is personal.

■ **On average, what percentage of your regular meetings is inspirational and what percentage is informational?**

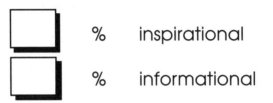

% inspirational

% informational

■ **How could you improve the format of your meetings? Give three suggestions.**

1. _____

2. _____

3. _____

■ **How could you celebrate successes in your organization or area?**

_____

_____

_____

_____

Towards the next step

So, to repeat, the seven soft-stuff staples are: clearly and confidently communicate your organization's purpose, vision and focus; use the tools of training and development; design working space that actually works; recognize the roles of a leader; measure creatively and meaningfully; can the complexity; and inspire others. Try to use all seven staples if you can. They are not the only tools you can use to deliver your organization's purpose, vision and focus, but they provide a strong foundation.

Equipped with these staples, the members of your organization, no matter what its size or makeup, should be able to fulfil your strategic plan. Although some staples may appear to be more applicable to companies than families, with a little creativity, most can be applied with equal effectiveness.

Even with the right soft stuff in place, however, there is still one thing separating you from success–behavior. The individuals within your organization must use the soft-stuff staples. They must put them into practise. Otherwise, all your time, effort and money is wasted.

So, ask yourself what behaviors you want your organization to exhibit–whether it's your relationship, family, neighborhood, city, department, wherever. That's what the next Footprint is all about. You will see the power of the soft stuff only when you use it to set standards for behaviors and then encourage and recognize those who actually display those behaviors. Then, ideas become action and action produces results. If you want results, they're only a Footstep away.

FOOTPRINT FIVE

Brilliancies in Behavior

Part I : Individual

An idealist believes the short run doesn't count. A cynic believes the long run doesn't matter. A realist believes that what is done or left undone in the short run determines the long run.

> SYDNEY J. HARRIS
> American newspaper
> columnist

We judge ourselves by what we feel capable of doing, while others judge us by what we have already done.

HENRY WADSWORTH LONGFELLOW
American author

Thanks to Footprints 1 through 4, we should now know why we're in the woods (purpose), who we want to be when we get out of the woods (vision), what direction we'll take (focus) and what mental and physical equipment we'll need to make the journey (the soft stuff). Now things get interesting. Now we're going to find out if we've got what it takes to ultimately succeed.

Our behavior, more than anything, determines the outcome of our adventures in life. Yes, outside factors can and do play a role–sometimes a major role. But far and away the biggest key to success is our actions–or inactions.

Footprints 1 through 4 largely involved some of the preparations we needed to make our journey through life. How we put these principles into practice determines whether we succeed. When the obstacles and challenges of life are staring us in the face, that is the moment of truth.

In this Footprint, as in others, we'll start with a discussion of the importance of behavior. Then, we'll go through the steps necessary for you to develop your own personal code of behavior.

To risk is to act, to act is to learn

When I was eight, I learned something about moments of truth. It changed my behavior.

My father bought me my first bicycle. For the life of me, I don't know why they design boys' bikes with a cross bar, but they do. Women's pleasure bikes aren't made that way, yet males would seem to be the ones with more to lose.

I also don't know why parents buy bikes so big for boys so small. Maybe it's to save money. That way, little tykes can grow into big bikes. At first though, big bikes don't allow little tykes to put both feet on the ground without being impaled on the cross bar.

Within minutes of presenting me with my new bike, my father took me out to show me how to ride it. To help me learn, he held onto the seat while running along beside me. All too soon I yelled: "Let go! I can do it by myself!" So, he let go.

My maiden ride was a rush. I was on my own–flying! After two or three minutes, I was a block or so from home. I decided it was time to get off. Suddenly, I realized I had not yet learned how to get off from a moving bicycle. I hadn't even read a book on cycling. I would have given every dime in my piggy bank for a chapter on "How to get off a moving bike" at that moment.

Life is like riding a bicycle. You don't fall off until you stop pedalling.

CLAUDE PEPPER
American Congressman

So how does one dismount, for the first time, without instruction, from a bike? Well, I slowed the beast down as much as possible by coasting. Then, with the gentle application of the pedal brakes, just as I was about to teeter over, I spread my legs and in total ignorance dropped onto the cross bar.

I have never felt such excruciating pain! My whole life flashed before me! The family jewels (small, but nevertheless with potential), received a blow never to be forgotten. I hugged the sidewalk, writhing.

A neighbor who'd seen what happened rushed to my aid, but there was nothing she could do. Anyone who has been in this predicament realizes that no amount of help (and how does one explain this to concerned parties?) can ease the agony. For what seems like an eternity, you are in a private purgatory.

209

The neighbor helped me up. I wanted to die. I struggled home, holding my privates and pushing the bike at the same time. (Try it sometime. It's not easy.)

The end of the road

The point of this story is simple, but important. Was it the last time I ever rode the bike? Certainly not! Was it the last time I hugged the sidewalk while riding my bike? Certainly not either!

Sometime later, I came around a corner too quickly on my bike and did a face plant on the back window of a parked car. It was sidewalk hugging time again! This time I staggered home with a crippled front wheel, a flattened face and crushed pride. But I rode again!

The message in this madness is we can all vividly recall instances in our lives when we didn't know how to behave perfectly. Remember learning how to walk? You probably don't, but you know you fell down a lot. If we had waited until the "perfect" time to learn how to walk, we would never have taken the first step.

Remember learning how to drive the family car? Were you perfect at it the first time? How about that first date? Smooth as silk?

If you think there are no new frontiers, watch a boy ring the front doorbell on his first date.

OLIN MILLER

We are all human. We aren't perfect. Yet this doesn't mean we should give up trying to live "perfect" lives. Just as the Japanese aspired to achieve zero defects in manufacturing, we can aspire to 100-per-cent success and happiness in all aspects of our lives.

Riding the new road to risk

The road to our goal begins with our first ride. Trying personal behavior principles is like learning how to ride a bike. We have to be willing to make a few mistakes before we master the skill. Over time, our actions will become automatic.

By definition, "practice" means attempting to improve at something by doing it repeatedly. But we don't need to practise in situations of high risk.

While we're talking to gas station attendants, for example, we can share our purpose, vision and focus. Or, if we wish, we can simply observe (not just see) them in their work, or listen to them (not just hear them). As we see the results–the positive effect we have on others and on ourselves–we can begin to transfer those behaviors into our personal lives.

Comfort zones

One of the reasons we fail to achieve our potential in life is we rarely stray outside our known parameters–our comfort zones. We say "we can't" do something new, but do we really mean "we won't"?

We have to get on the bike and take a trip (or fall)–no matter how hesitant we might be. Any action that could provide us with some degree of momentum, experience and learning is far better than waiting for that perfect moment to begin. The operative word is momentum. Why? Because as Newton so well determined:

A body at rest tends to stay at rest. A body in motion tends to stay in motion.

NEWTON'S first Law of Motion,
The Principle of Inertia

If we are motionless, it is very difficult to experience or learn anything.

211

The success in failure

In learning, an attempted effort is more important than perfection. This is because attempted efforts ultimately enable us to approach perfection.

A child walks this talk better than anyone else. Some adults seem to forget it. Failures, large or small, eventually contribute to success.

> *There is the greatest practical benefit in making a few failures early in life.*
>
> THOMAS H. HUXLEY
> English biologist

> *Failure is the opportunity to begin again more intelligently.*
>
> Henry Ford
> Automobile manufacturer

Failure can be seen in two ways–as failure or as opportunity.

As astronaut Neil Armstrong so aptly said when he first set foot on the moon: **"One small step for man; one giant leap for mankind."** The goal of putting a man on the moon was not achieved by dreamers who simply dreamed. It was achieved by dreamers who took action, who made mistakes, accepted failure as part of the program and drove their dreams to reality.

We seem to want success without failure. We want the pay-out without the pay-in–the achievement without the effort. I think it's a bit like wanting to ride a bicycle without ever hugging the sidewalk. It's ideal, but it's not realistic.

> *He who never made a mistake never made a discovery.*
>
> SAMUEL SMILES
> Scottish author

Take a moment now and stop reading. Think back over some of your successes in life. Ask yourself how they were achieved. Close your eyes.

▲　　▲　　▲　　▲

So, how did you achieve your successes? If you answer, "by learning from previous mistakes," then give yourself credit.

One of the psychological tricks I use to overcome fear is to ask myself if the potential outcome is life-threatening. If it isn't, then I am willing to try. Too often, we feel our actions may be "career-threatening." But by doing nothing, we become equally threatened. Many of those I know who do take action believe they would rather go down in the middle of the action with both guns blasting than be gunned down from the sidelines having never fired a shot.

To Laugh is to Risk Appearing the Fool
To Weep is to Risk Appearing Sentimental
To Reach Out for Another is to Risk Involvement
To Expose Feelings is to Risk Exposing Our True
　　Selves
To Place Our Ideas, Our Dreams Before the
Crowd is to Risk Loss
To Love is to Risk Not Being Loved in Return
To Live is to Risk Dying
To Hope is to Risk Despair
To Try is to Risk Failure
But to Risk We Must, for the Greatest Hazard
　　in Life is to Risk Nothing
The Man, the Woman, Who Risks Nothing
Does Nothing, Has Nothing, Is Nothing.

ANONYMOUS

213

Using fantasy over fear

Write down two or three things you've always wanted to do. Let your mind go. Then write down how you will "Go for it!"

I've always wanted to...

_____

_____

_____

_____

I'll start to realize my goal today by...

_____

_____

_____

_____

The power of perception

The first thing to understand about failure is that what we imagine might happen is generally far worse than what occurs. That's because our perception of risk is rarely congruous with the reality of risk. The key factor is perception–our perception.

Perception is within our control. I remember climbing once with an experienced mountaineer. After an evening of extremely high winds, much of our equipment was blown away. We spent the night literally clinging to the saddle between two mountains. I perceived danger. So did my companion.

214

In the morning, when the weather cleared and the winds diminished, my companion admitted we had been under "real risk." I thought all risk was "real risk." I was wrong.

My partner explained when he taught students about mountaineering, he deliberately placed them in situations of "perceived risk." Although they felt threatened, they were actually in little danger because proper safety systems were in place. The situation was designed to give them an idea of what could happen. Often, our perceptions lead us to believe we are truly at risk. Sometimes we are, but often, we are not. It is our fear, lack of knowledge and, sometimes, lack of self-confidence that can lead us to perceive that risk exists. The real risk, our perception, can overpower us to the point of inaction.

A child's perception of risk

When we were children, we had few perceptions of risk. We approached each new challenge at "face value." If we were perched at the top of a hill on our toboggan and the hill was steep, we'd let 'er fly. We didn't perceive danger because we had never experienced injury.

> *When we think of our child we think of that which is good, unspoiled, open to life and eager to participate. A child is one who engages life directly. Children do not so easily get lost in analysis or in projecting a certain image of themselves to others. To reclaim our inner child is to regain that kind of innocence.* [1]

> JEFFREY D. IMBACH
> Pastor, author,
> spiritual director

215

Wouldn't it be great if we could keep behaving the way we did as kids–seeing only the positive in a situation and disregarding the negative? The problem is that as we get older, we are programmed to avoid risk.

As children, our parents tell us what we're not allowed to do. In an effort to protect us, they attempt to reduce the risk in our lives. When we leave home, our peers and society reduce our risk-taking even more. They make fun of us when we fall, or discourage us from trying again when we make mistakes. Our society discourages childlike behavior. At best, it is considered immature. At worst, it is considered foolish.

If we are to succeed, this perception of risk has got to stop–or at least we must begin to try to change it. To the person who insists "Grow up!" I say "Think big! Act small!" In an intriguing way, to be successful, we have to revert to our childhood. We have to take and encourage more risk because risks, properly taken, produce growth. Not taking risks doesn't produce anything except the same old thing–business as usual.

216

When you're through changing, you're through.

BRUCE BARTON
American advertising
executive, author

The essence of action

If we want results different from those we've been getting, we need to act differently. But there's a problem. The more times we attempt different behaviors, the more times we'll likely fail. Society's response to this is swift and judgmental–it's not good for the bottom line.

I disagree. I think failing *is* good for the bottom line– in the long run. If, and only if, we change our attitudes.

Behavior produces attitude

In my work, I have noticed **behavior produces attitude, but attitude does not necessarily produce behavior.** Psychologists may not agree. But if you want to change your attitude about something, you don't just sit down and decide to do it. You may decide you'd like to do it, but it is the actual act of doing it that produces a change in your attitude.

When I conduct management training seminars, I note with interest the positive effect jogging can have on participants. In the beginning, there are always some individuals who are neutral or negative about fitness. Many members of my executive seminars have never run a mile in their lives. Within weeks, up to 20 per cent of them are running 5 and even 10 miles! They are amazed. This single event boosts them to a whole new level of self-understanding.

One of the fascinating by-products of this realization is that they suddenly become more proactive in the management training sessions themselves.

217

I believe their behavior changes because:

- through shared physical activity they become more at ease with fellow participants and

- they begin to realize they really *can* achieve something they never thought possible if they only did it.

Essentially, any human activity offers three different kinds of benefits: the rewards that come from performance, or the external results of the action; those produced by the experience of performing the activity; and the learning or growth that takes place during the action. [2]

W. TIMOTHY GALLWEY
Sports psychologist, author

Don't let me give you the impression I make jogging a mandatory part of all my seminars. I do not. But jogging does, I hope, illustrate a very important facet about ourselves–that if we want to change the attitudes of those around us, we must first influence them to change their behavior. Changing attitudes may not produce action.

A change in behavior for the better

I promised you action and I'm going to deliver. How do we become more action-oriented? How do we break out of thought and behavioral patterns that limit us? There is a way.

Your guidelines to greatness

In "The Soft Stuff," we loaded our packs and minds with the gear needed to succeed. Now, we're going to talk about the attitudes that will keep our actions consistently effective. We're going to talk about action attitudes like risk-taking, courage, perseverance, endurance, commitment, enthusiasm and toughness. If these seem too existential to you at the moment, I again ask for your patience. We'll get to the heart of the matter in the next few paragraphs.

The military and some organizations call these attitudes "codes of conduct." I call them "codes of behavior." Whatever you call them, they can make the difference between just talking our walk or actually walking our talk.

Procedure

Look back to your purpose and vision Steps. In each Footprint, you were asked to write down a list of words to help you develop your personal purpose and vision statements.

Bring forward all the words, even the ones you selected for your purpose and vision statements. In any order, write them here:

Elements of my code of behavior

_____

_____

_____

_____

_____

Let's suppose your list includes enthusiasm, love, caring, sharing, pride, continuous improvement, and open-mindedness.

Using one word at a time, write a short sentence using each of these words. Each sentence should describe a behavior you would like to exhibit. The sentences you might develop from the words above are:

- To be **enthusiastic** in everything I do.

- To be a **loving** parent to my children.

- To **care** deeply about how I act/behave in work and play.

- To **share** my feelings with others.

- To take **pride** in everything I do.

- To look for opportunities to **continuously improve** myself on a day-to-day basis.

- To be childlike in my attitude so I am **open** to new thoughts and ideas.

Now, in a similar way, use your own words from the list made above to develop sentences:

My personal code of behavior: Touchstones to the top

_____

_____

_____

_____

_____

A code of behavior in practice

As I said in the Introduction, the ideas presented in this book can be applied to almost any activity in your life–from writing a book, to building a business, or even weaving a basket. A code of behavior can be applied to any process that benefits from a careful, step-by-step approach. Thus, although you may find yourself thinking about the larger levels of your life as you read this book, you can also use the Six Steps at the smaller levels.

For example, while we wrote this book, Alan and I constantly referred to a sheet of paper on which we had written the purpose, vision and focus for the book, along with our code of behavior. Included in this Code of Behavior was:

> To remain **open to** each other's ideas.
> To treat each other with **mutual respect**
> at all times.
> To have **open and frank dialogue.**
> To **accept criticism.**
> To be **patient** with one another.
> To **continuously improve** the product and
> the production methods.
> And above all, to...
>
> **Never, never, never quit.**

You might wish to consider such an idea. Or, to be even more effective, you might wish to write down your purpose, vision and focus on one sheet of paper and your code of behavior on another, and frame and display them in a prominent place in your home or office.

Applying your code of behavior to your life

There's no sense in developing a tool unless we know how to use it. Let's suppose that one of the elements of your code of behavior is "To have courage." That sounds good, but it's rather ambiguous.

It's surprisingly easy to apply this element to our lives. When we feel ourselves giving into fear, we must remind ourselves to have courage. We must be brave.

Likewise, if one of the elements of our code of behavior is "To be enthusiastic," then we need to give ourselves a kick in the pants when we're starting to get down.

Procedure

One by one, write down each element of your code of behavior below. Beside each element, write down what the element means to you and how you think it could be applied to your life at two levels: generally and specifically.

Elements of my code of behavior

_____

_____

_____

_____

_____

_____

222

What it means to me

_____

_____

_____

_____

_____

_____

How I can apply it to my life generally

_____

_____

_____

_____

_____

_____

_____

_____

_____

_____

_____

How I can apply it to my life specifically

The importance of your code of behavior

At first glance, your code of behavior may not seem significant. Actually, it is very significant. It is not intended to tell us what to do. As we all live such different lives, it is impossible for any process to have all the "action answers." But your code of behavior can tell you how to do things. And, if you think about it, what we do is not nearly as important as how we do it.

Let me illustrate. Every year, millions of couples decide they'd like to renovate their home. Whether they do it themselves or contract the work to someone else, the result is usually the same–stress on the relationship.

The couple works furiously to overcome many pressures–financial, organizational and logistical. The builders make any number of changes–installing new heating ducts and new fixtures, even knocking down walls, making additions and replacing windows. The couple knows, or at least think they know, what they need to do. Every evening and sometimes every day, many young couples work up to 18 hours at a time on such projects. As the work progresses, their relationship may get into trouble.

These interpersonal problems, I believe, have more to do with improper personal focus and code of behavior than with the considerable stress often associated with home renovation. In the process of sprucing up the house, they forget the home.

If **what** you want to do is build a house, then your code of behavior might be: *(call this code of behavior 1)*

- To **plan** properly.
- To **use** the best materials at the lowest cost.
- To **build** wisely.
- To **subcontract** the complex work.
- To enjoy **myself.**

But if you want to build a home, that's a different story. Then, your code of behavior should focus on **how** to do it. Your code of behavior might be: *(call this code of behavior 2)*

- To **love** my partner.
- To **share** in the construction of our home.
- To treat each other with mutual **respect.**
- To mediate disagreements in a manner that puts the **relationship** first and the house second.
- To have fun **together.**

Clearly, the code of behavior for building a house and building a home are very different. If you're trying to "do the right things" in building your house, then code of behavior 1 might work. But if you're trying to build a home, then code of behavior 2 may help you approach the task with the right frame of mind.

"Doing things right" involves more than just bottom line results–in this case, the construction of a beautiful house. It involves taking all the proper qualitative steps to ensure that the quantitative results are also achieved.

In our journey from infancy to proficiency, whether in house building, business building or life building, if we follow our code of behavior we should be able to stay on track. It should help us during moments of decision. That's doing things right and doing the right things. It's knowing what has to be done and knowing how to do it.

Exercising your right to choose

Now that you have seen how to apply your code of behavior to areas in your life in which you must make a decision, you are ready to go ahead, right? Well, maybe not. You may know what to do, but actually doing it is another thing.

To help you along, write down three areas in your life in which you must make a decision or about which you are currently indecisive. Beside them, list the elements of your code of behavior that can be applied to the situation.

Area of decision:
Applicable elements of my code

_____

_____

_____

_____

_____

_____

Three obstacles to attaining your code of behavior

Regardless of what activity you may be considering, there are at least two major obstacles to attaining your code of behavior. One is fear. The other is the "I've Made It" morass.

Fear

> *Experience is not what happens to you; it is what you do with what happens to you.*
>
> ALDOUS HUXLEY
> English author, critic

The number one thing that prevents us from sticking to our code of behavior and achieving better individual bottom lines, I believe, is fear. When we try to build a house, learn to play a new musical instrument or speak in public, for example, we often hesitate because we're afraid of making mistakes. Fear stops us–fear of failure, fear of the unknown and fear of ridicule. This applies to all activities in which we become involved, whether personally or professionally.

Professionally, financial fear stops us from quitting jobs in which we are unhappy. Fear of being fired or rejected prevents us from making unauthorized decisions at work. Fear of bankruptcy stops us from starting up our own business. Fear of the unknown blocks us from applying for a transfer at work. Fear stops us from speaking to our significant others because we're afraid they won't understand. Fear of rejection prevents us from entering into new or deeper relationships and, if we are men, fear of being "unmanly" or "too womanly" stops us from showing our emotions.

227

Putting your finger on your fears

Where has fear entered your life? Is it financial worry, legal concerns, relationship problems, family crises or health issues? Write down your fears and number them. It may be unpleasant, but find the courage to do it. Beside each number, with your code of behavior in mind, write down what action you can take to alleviate each of your fears.

Personal fears

1. _____

2. _____

3. _____

Applicable elements of my code of behavior

1. _____

2. _____

3. _____

Action

1. _____

2. _____

3. _____

I wish I could give you a neat little system to overcome fear. It kills countless dreams, even before the first step is taken. In fact, it usually prevents the first step from ever being taken. Thus, all the steps that could have followed never take place.

In this book, I will give you as many tools, procedures and systems as I can to help you in your journey. But **you** must find the courage to continue. **You** must fight fear. **You** must have faith.

The "I've made it" morass!

When you stop learning, stop listening, stop looking and asking questions, always new questions, then it is time to die.

LILLIAN SMITH
American author

Fear is not the only major obstacle to achieving your code of behavior. Another is the "I've Made It" morass.

I believe for us to be successful, there should be no difference between how we act at home and how we act outside our homes. Both should follow our code of behavior. Thus, there should be no "compartmentalization" of our behavior.

If we snap at a flight attendant, for example, chances are we'll snap at our friends or significant others. Likewise, if we talk down to a waitress, chances are we'll talk down to a neighbor.

Dale Carnegie and other self-improvement courses describe four levels of behavior:
1. Unconsciously incompetent
2. Consciously incompetent
3. Consciously competent
4. Unconsciously competent[3]

229

When a person first becomes a parent, for example, they have no idea whether or not they are competent. For the first little while (and sometimes a lot longer), they flail in the dark. They are *unconsciously incompetent.* If they are not a natural parent, they soon (but not always) *consciously* realize they are *incompetent* and, therefore, need help. So, they seek out a friend or fellow parent. In time, their level of competency improves and they become *consciously competent.* They know this because they begin to realize recognition for their efforts. They receive verbal praise, hugs, or other such displays of affection from their spouse and/or children.

If, at this point, parents decide they're good enough, they become complacent. That's when they fall into the morass. Unconsciously, they believe they're competent. They are, but very soon thereafter, they are not. To grow, we must keep pedalling. When we stop pedalling, we fall.

The crux of the matter is this: the moment we attain level 4 and become unconsciously competent in any activity in life, we soon revert to level 1–being unconsciously incompetent. Or...

> *When you're green, you grow. When you're ripe, you rot.*
>
> RAY KROC
> Founder, McDonald's Corp.

To grow and keep growing in the long term, we must consistently revisit our purpose, vision, focus, soft stuff and code of behavior to ensure we're on target. If we've achieved our initial objectives, we need to set new ones.

The point is that in order to achieve excellence, our behavior must be consistent in a positive way. We must act today to live for tomorrow. And, we must act with honesty and integrity every day in every way with everyone. To behave otherwise is to virtually assure long-term failure.

230

Catching complacency

Write down those areas in your life in which you might have become complacent or are in danger of doing so. Are you becoming complacent with yourself, your family or your work? If your list is blank, that's great. But have you stopped growing anywhere? Beside each area, write down how you might begin to rectify the situation.

Areas of possible complacency

_____

_____

_____

_____

_____

Actions required

_____

_____

_____

_____

231

How we learn

Enough about obstacles such as fear and complacency. Let's talk about opportunities–the ways in which we can seize the day. We learn to succeed in three basic ways–through thought, imitation and action. Thought enables us to learn through reasoning; imitation allows us to learn by mirroring others; and action enables us to learn by doing. All are powerful learning methods, but it is only through action that thought and imitation can take life.

> *I hear and I forget. I see and I remember.*
> *I do and I understand.*
>
> CONFUCIUS
> Chinese philosopher, teacher

How you're presently learning

List at least five of the most significant activities in which you are currently engaged. Consider self, work, relationships, leisure, clubs, associations, health, spirituality, finances, family or anything else significant to you. Beside each, write down whether you are involved through thought (e.g., reading), imitation (e.g., role modelling) or action (e.g., doing).

Activity
Nature of my involvement (thought, imitation or action)

_____

_____

_____

_____

Ideally, all your activities should be in or moving towards the "action" stage.

From your list above, develop another list below. Enter all those activities currently in the "thought" or "imitation" stage. Explain how you intend to put them into action.

Activities now in the "thought" or "imitation" stage

_____

_____

_____

_____

_____

How I will "activate" them

_____

_____

_____

_____

_____

233

Beating back the bears

If we constantly return to our touchstones, our code of behavior, we need not concern ourselves with obstacles to the degree we once did. Obstacles will always be present, but the degree to which they are a threat will be markedly reduced if we follow our code. Together with our purpose, vision, focus and soft stuff, our code of behavior will give us all the tools we need to survive and succeed.

When two actors try out for the same part in a play by delivering the same lines, what they say is exactly the same, but how they say it isn't. The director senses the difference and ultimately, so does the audience. Actors call this "interpreting" lines.

We are all actors in life and we all "interpret" our situations based on our code of behavior or lack of it. We are also the writers, directors, producers, stage managers and set designers in our own play. In fact, we're a composite of everyone who works in the theatre–with one very big difference. We're not play acting. Our drama is real. There are no dress rehearsals. Every night is opening–or closing–night.

How we treat our fellow actors–our friends, associates and significant others, even that waitress or gas station attendant–determines the success of our entire play. Every time we interact with others, we are performing a scene from our lives. Each scene builds to an act of one day and each day builds to a finale. Life is not one long play, but a series of short scenes of one act.

It's not just what we do on stage and off that counts, but how we do it–how we interact with others, how we say our lines, how we react in scenes of suspense, drama, anger, even tedium. If we succumb to stage fright and fail to act, the outcome of our actions or inactions will be inevitable. But if, instead, we return to our touchstones and act according to our code of behavior, we may be impressed with the results.

*We are given one life and the decision is ours
whether to wait for circumstances to make up
our mind or whether we act, and in acting, live.*

OMAR BRADLEY
General, U.S. Army

How we act each day of our life–how we behave–will bring others to their feet cheering for us or send them stomping out of our lives in disappointment and disgust. But before the curtain calls, we will have an opportunity to measure our progress–if we know something about our last line– **The Bottom Line**.

FOOTPRINT FIVE

Brilliancies in Behavior

Leadership appears to be the art of getting others to...do something you are convinced should be done.

VANCE PACKARD
American journalist

Leadership is an action, not a word.

RICHARD P. COOLEY
American banker

With the soft stuff, we've loaded our packs and minds with the physical and psychological equipment needed to succeed. Now we'll address the behaviors that will keep our actions consistently effective.

In many organizations, there is a discrepancy between what leaders say is important and how members actually act. So, there is inconsistency between organizational thought and individual action. In a corporation, upper management may determine that "customer service" is one of the organization's points of focus, but the desired behavior does not result. This usually occurs because the soft stuff isn't present or isn't properly implemented. Similarly, in a family, the parents may take a strong stance against drug abuse, but persist in abusing alcohol or cigarettes–the old "do as I say, not as I do" routine.

I believe it is any organization's responsibility to develop and enforce a "Code of Behavior" for its members to follow. It is imperative that a list of expected behaviors be established. Once determined, these behaviors should be shown and explained to everyone who wishes to join the organization or stay in it. These behaviors should form part of every employee's performance appraisal review.

Getting with the program

Whether it's through training programs, informative meetings, pep rallies, or formal performance appraisal sessions, the principles of effective behavior must be continually communicated and reinforced at all levels of the organization.

This applies to everyone from security guards to flight attendants, auto mechanics, salespeople, or CEOs. The same principles must apply–consistently and with full accountability.

The biggest cause of mismanagement in organizations is failing to clearly communicate expectations. Simply telling people the end result you desire– the bottom line–is necessary, but not sufficient. Thus, it's not enough to say to a security guard: "Keep this parking spot open," or to a flight attendant: "De-plane the passengers," or to a manager: "Just do your job." You have to explain why and when to keep parking spots open, and more importantly, when not to. Similarly, if you're a flight crew director, you have to show how to empty the plane, especially when problems arise. Everyone has to know the exact expectations of "the job."

As a leader, you must coach, encourage, teach and inspire others to take part and be a part of the journey. Most employees look to their leader as their main source of information–especially for information about what is expected of them as employees.[1]

I also believe organizations need to establish a code of ethics to which their members must adhere. These two codes, behavioral and ethical, take the guessing game out of members' minds. With them in place, everyone knows how to act, whether in a crisis or during humdrum, everyday living.

The code of behavior we're going to talk about in this Footprint includes such things as risk-taking, courage, honesty, perseverance, endurance, commitment, enthusiasm and toughness. The military and other organizations call these principles "codes of conduct." I call them "organizational codes of behavior." Whatever you call them, they can make the difference between talking our walk and walking our talk.

The difference between walking and talking

Some organizational leaders don't appear to care about anything but the bottom line. These kinds of leaders won't last any more. Why? Because they're living in the past–in the era of capital and technology-driven thinking. They've missed the relationship revolution and have become dinosaurs. If they don't adapt, they'll perish. The sooner leaders wake up to larger, global responsibilities and lead on the basis of people and behavioral principles, not solely for profit, the sooner the whole world will improve.

I once asked an employee in an organization going through major structural and operational changes how things were progressing. All members had taken a course on how decision making and risk taking would now be part of everyone's responsibility. This was seen as a radical shift from the previous "top down" management philosophy. The employee's reply was revealing: "I won't know how this program is working until we see how management reacts when someone makes a mistake."

Slogans, rhetoric and flag-waving won't make the soft stuff deliver for you. I have seen individuals within organizations spit out impressive belief statements, but such announcements are hollow when you look at their behavior. Purpose, vision and focus only become powerful when behaviorial statements are reflected in action. Well-guided and accountable behavior boosts the bottom line. People produce profits.

How to develop an organizational code of behavior

Just as we have traced results back to behavior, we will now trace behavior back to the principles that underlie it.

239

This is roughly akin to deciding we'd like to build a house (bottom line), setting a timetable for completing the various construction stages (measurements), determining how the nails must be driven and the woodcuts made (the soft stuff and behavior) and then...deciding how to keep ourselves motivated and on track while the work progresses (behavioral principles).

The elements of your organization's code of behavior will act as touchstones to return to when you are faced with decisions. For example, if we decide to improve customer service, one of the behaviors we may determine is important is: "Remain cool at all costs, remember the customer is always right."

What happens if something goes wrong, the customer gets upset and starts taking it out on us? What happens if a team member fails us and puts us on the spot with a customer? Our soft stuff training tells us *what to do.* Our code of behavior tells us *how we should do it.* It should help us retain our confidence, maintain our courage and continue our journey amid adversity.

Time and time again in life, these psychological principles make the difference between failure and success. Some of the most admired organizations in the world–Johnson & Johnson, Merck Pharmaceutical, Hewlett-Packard, Levi Strauss and Wal-Mart–have built their success on blending human values with the hard business assets of capital and technology.

To downplay the importance of principle-centered leadership (to quote a phrase coined by Dr. Stephen Covey, author of *Principle-Centered Leadership* and *The 7 Habits of Highly Effective People*) is to overlook one of the most fundamental principles of high achievement.

Step One in developing your organizational code of behavior:

List the significant factors in your code

Look back to your organization's purpose and vision statements in Footsteps 1 and 2. To produce those statements, you wrote a list of key words. Then, you used three or four of them to form your purpose and vision statements.

Bring forward all of those words now, even the ones you selected for your purpose and vision statements. In any order, write them here:

The key factors in my
organization's code of behavior

_____

_____

_____

_____

_____

_____

 Step Two in developing your organizational code of behavior:

Build the code

Let's suppose your list above includes these words: enthusiasm, teamwork, simplicity, service, innovation, acceptance, leadership, pride, continuous improvement and open-mindedness.

241

You might develop sentences like the following from the above words:

- To be **enthusiastic** in everything we do.
- To be **team** players.
- To strive for **simplicity** in all activities relating to **serving** one another.
- To nurture **innovation** through the **acceptance** of outrageousness in the ideas we generate.
- To display **leadership** when appropriate.
- To take **pride** in our work.
- To look for opportunities to **continuously improve** our organization every day.
- To maintain an attitude of **open-mindedness** to new thoughts and ideas—even when they may at first appear ridiculous.

As in the above examples, use each of your words in a sentence. Each sentence should describe a behavior you would like to see members of your organization exhibit.

My organization's code of behavior
Statements for which we will be held accountable

_____

_____

_____

_____

_____

_____

Codes of behavior at work

PEROT SYSTEMS

Ross Perot, a former member of the General Motors (GM) board of directors, established a code of behavior when he left GM to start a new company, Perot Systems. It was as follows:

We will

- Have only one class of team member–a full partner.

- Recognize and reward excellence while the individual is still sweating from their efforts. (Remember "Employee of the Moment"?)

- Build and maintain a spirit of "one for all and all for one."

- Hold team members accountable for results, with...great flexibility in deciding how to achieve results (and) with a clear understanding that ethical standards must never be compromised.

- Eliminate any opportunity for people to succeed by merely looking good.

- Promote solely on merit.

Perot went further with his organizational code of behavior. He made a list of unacceptable behaviors. You may wish to do so as well. It was as follows:

We will not tolerate anyone who

- Acts in a manner which discredits this organization.

- Discriminates with regard to race, religion, sex, or any other reason.

- Looks down on others.

- Becomes a corporate politician.

243

- Tries to move ahead at the expense of others.
- Uses illegal drugs.[2]

CRESTAR ENERGY INC.

Crestar, an energy company in Calgary, Canada, developed something they called their "Guiding Principles." It consisted of both their purpose and vision statements as well as their "Code of Conduct":

Our conduct is fundamental to achieving our purpose:

- We treat each other with respect.

- We are open, honest, and trustworthy.

- We encourage everyone to take risks, make decisions, exercise initiative, and never be afraid to make mistakes.

- We seek a balance in our professional and personal lives.

- We recognize and celebrate our achievements.

- We foster mutually beneficial relationships with our shareholders and business associates.

- We demonstrate responsible citizenship and commitment to safety, health and the environment.[3]

GENERAL ELECTRIC

General Electric's 1989 Annual Report includes a paragraph that embodies an aspiration for a set of behaviors. If emulated, these behaviors should drive employees towards the organization's purpose and vision:

We've found that people perform better, even heroically, when they see that what they do every day makes a difference.

When they see that when they are allowed to make real contributions to winning, they quickly develop increased self-confidence. That self-confidence in turn promotes simplicity–of action, of design, of process and of communication because there is no longer a psychic need to wrap oneself in the complexity, trappings, and jargon that, in a bureaucracy, signify sophistication and stature. That simplicity will radically increase the speed of our businesses and their ability to react to a world whose pace of change will become astonishing in the 1990s. Speed, simplicity, and self-confidence will be the operative characteristics of the winning companies of the 1990s and beyond...

Far-fetched? Fuzzy? Soft? Naive? Not a bit. This is the type of liberated, involved, excited, boundary-less culture that is present in successful start-up enterprises. It is unheard of in many our size; but we want it, and we are determined we will have it. [4]

B.C. HYDRO

British Columbia Hydro, a company on Canada's west coast, has established what it calls five key corporate values [focus points]: integrity, teamwork, empowerment, commitment, and innovation.

"These values," the company writes, "were translated into understandable behavioral terms that had meaning to our workforce. "

They were:
- our actions should match our words
- we should work together toward shared goals
- our enthusiasm should be contagious
- we should try new ideas
- we should learn from our mistakes

These values were called climate goals. Each management team developed its own business unit strategy and at regular meetings, the team assessed its ability to achieve its goals. That assessment included the team's ability to manage its climate. [5]

The results of B.C. Hydro's thinking have been remarkable. The utility was recognized by the Institute of Public Administration of Canada in their 1991 Awards for Innovative Management, and the company's chairman received the prestigious Vanier Medal for organizational excellence.

CANADIAN HUNTER

A Calgary-based energy company, Canadian Hunter, has set out its guiding principles:

We strive to be:
- The Best Oil Company in Canada
- Not the biggest
- Not the richest
- But the best, the most excellent

The Best Company to work for, by providing:
- Dignity and growth for the individual
- Opportunity to contribute
- Generous compensation
- First priority to the family
- Fun on the job

The Best People, through:
- Meticulous selection
- Training and development
- Trust and respect for each other

The Best Citizens in the Community, by:

- Giving
- Leading
- Being an Example

We are all in this together. It is our company. The over-riding goal is to discover and produce energy. In doing that, we create wealth where none existed before. Ultimately, the nation's people are enriched. [6]

A code of behavior for meetings

A code of behavior can be applied to activities much smaller than corporate principles. To eliminate unnecessary meetings, Xerox asked each member of its organization to ask themselves two questions:

- Who is the customer for this meeting?
- What are the customer's requirements?

Any meetings that could not identify a customer were cancelled. [7]

For those meetings not cancelled, the following code of behavior or "Gatekeeping Guidelines" was established and constantly reviewed during the meeting:

- Be open to and encourage ideas
- Look for merit in the ideas
- Strive for win-win ideas
- Listen non-defensively
- Pay attention and avoid side conversations
- Limit war stories (or "remember whens")
- Look for facts
- Help to summarize
- Each member is responsible for the team's progress [8]

How to use your code of behavior

There's no sense in developing a tool unless you know how to use it. Now that you've put together your organization's code of behavior, you need to know how to maximize its effectiveness in your day-to-day work. The next few pages will focus on this.

Let's suppose one of the elements of your code of behavior is to "encourage simplicity in the way we work." It's easy to apply this principle. When we see our systems beginning to choke our operations, we must remind ourselves to keep things simple–for everyone inside and outside our organization. We must ask ourselves at every meeting and before every action whether we are making things simpler. If we aren't, we need to rethink what we are doing.

Likewise, if one of the elements of our code of behavior is "to be enthusiastic," then when things aren't going our way, we need to catch ourselves before we become negative.

Let's suppose your organization has decided to reduce its labour costs. If one of the elements of your organization's code of behavior is to "treat one another with respect and dignity," then perhaps it becomes important to look at other options besides layoffs. These might include such things as across-the-board salary cuts or job sharing. Members might be asked to suggest cost cutting ideas. Respect and dignity mean empowerment and accountability for everyone.

Or, if an organization is contemplating a merger, is that change, as is the case in Canadian Hunter's code of behavior, designed to make the organization the best, or simply the biggest?

Only by constantly monitoring our thoughts, attitudes and actions can we ever hope to achieve our ultimate goals.

248

Organizations without imbedded codes of behavior

I want to share with you three brief stories that I feel graphically illustrate the relationship between individual behavior and organizational excellence. The first involves a misguided security guard, the second, a less-than-congenial flight attendant and the third, a confused middle manager. All highlight the importance of producing proper action through an organizational code of behavior.

THE CASE OF THE MISGUIDED SECURITY GUARD

A colleague of mine once worked for a large firm. He was asked to hand-deliver a purchase order for $24,000 to one of the organization's suppliers. The supplier claimed to pride itself in customer service.

When the colleague got to the supplier's building, he drove into the parking lot and pulled into the parking spot nearest the front door. A security guard immediately approached him. Just as he was getting out, the guard said sternly: "I'm sorry sir, but you'll have to move your car."

My colleague showed him the $24,000 purchase order. He started to explain that he would just dash in to deliver the order.

The guard didn't wait for him to finish.

"I said, 'MOVE IT!'"

Undeterred, my colleague tried to continue.

"Listen buddy," the guard said threateningly, "just what don't you understand about 'move your car'?"

In frustration, my colleague got back into his car and drove away. He moved his car all right–five blocks down the street to one of the supplier's competitors. There, my friend delivered the $24,000 purchase order. He never went back to the original supplier. Nor did he ever bother telling the original supplier what had happened.

249

Some may argue that the security guard was just doing his job. Others may say my colleague acted too harshly in cancelling all future business. Yet studies show that the main reason customers change products or services is due to the indifference of one or more employees.[9]

Our world is highly competitive. What we can do, someone else can often do just as well. If you think otherwise, trouble may be just around the corner–and down the block.

By keeping the parking space clear, the security guard was "doing things right." He was following orders and being efficient. However, he sure wasn't doing the right things. Although he may have thought he was being efficient, he wasn't being effective. Effective behavior is more important than efficient behavior because it produces the best possible outcome. Efficient behavior only seeks a swift outcome.

The organization for which the guard worked did not only lose a $24,000 purchase order that day. It lost all of that customer's successive business as well–an additional $100,000 in annual revenue in this case. Worse still, the president may never know why the business was lost.

Organizations, as I've said in earlier Footprints, are made up of individuals. If they hope to achieve superior service, or any other organizational ideal, they must train their members to behave in ways which will deliver superior service. This may strike you as common sense. This may not: The guard probably wasn't at fault.

The relationship among purpose, vision, focus, the soft stuff and behavior

What do you think the guard's purpose, vision or focus was? If you think it was: "To protect my parking spaces from anyone who doesn't 'belong,'" you're probably right. His purpose, vision or focus did not include anything about customer service.

His goal was to protect territory–ironically, that territory was probably the president's parking stall. If you were the company president, what would you do? Fire the guard? Discipline him? I sincerely hope you would not condone his behavior!

Regardless, you'd probably want to ask the guard a few questions. You might want to discover why he acted the way he did.

Some presidents would fire the guard. The smarter ones would recognize it was their own fault. The guard was not adequately trained. He needed to understand that his total job included serving those who wanted to use the parking spaces. He also needed to understand the difference he could make to the success of the organization.

With proper training, the guard might display different behavior, by asking: "Good day, sir, what can I do to help you today?" When the customer explained he was there to deliver a purchase order, the guard could have offered to either temporarily guard "his" customer's car, or take the purchase order in himself.

In addition to demonstrating how individual behavior can affect organizational bottom lines, this story also emphasizes a major point made at the beginning of Footprint 4–soft stuff. The key to enjoying successful organizational behavior is building strong relationships both outside and inside the organization. Thus, a guard should have a relationship with the organization for which he works. Likewise, he should be trained to react to the individual, not the issue; the person, not the parking space.

Relationships encompass more than friendships or business associations developed over long periods of time. They involve any interaction we have with other people. It might be something as apparently insignificant as how you deal with a sales clerk. Even the most mundane interaction with someone can turn into a relationship of sorts. Without proper behavior, however, communication eventually stops.

COME FLY WITH ME

Given the nature of their business, airlines should be well schooled in the art of behavioral management, especially in a crisis. There are few businesses in which safety is such a high concern. Most of the crises in air travel, however, have nothing to do with weather, pilots, crashes or technical malfunctions. Like all service industries, they have to do with serving people.

I was travelling by plane when I witnessed a classic case of inadequate behavior under stress. Despite this particular airline's impressive claims about the importance of customer service, it was not transforming its ideals into employee attitude or behavior (at least not in this case.)

While de-planing from the front of the aircraft, a fellow passenger and I noticed another business traveller nearby who was very upset. Apparently, his carry-on suit bag was not at the front of the plane where he had stored it during boarding.

The cabin attendant explained that the crew had taken some of the suit bags to the back of the aircraft there having been insufficient room at the front.

"If you'll just stand aside and let everyone off," said the flight attendant, "I'll go and get your suit bag for you when the plane is clear. Is that satisfactory?"

His icy response unnerved the crew and sent a shudder up and down our collective spines.

"No, that is not satisfactory to me!" he snapped. "I want my suit bag–now!"

At this point, the flight attendant's courteous manner went out the door. Rather than maintaining her professionalism, she reacted emotionally.

"Well, what do you expect me to do?" the attendant exclaimed. "Fight all of these passengers to get to the back of the plane for your suit bag?"

Sensing that World War III was impending, I hurried off the plane just as the attendant and the passenger brought out the verbal artillery before some 200 departing passengers. As you may know, the cabin crew usually lines up beside the exits to bid goodbye to passengers as they get off. As soon as this exchange started, the crew retreated into the cockpit and closed the door.

I couldn't blame them. To that point in the flight, the crew had done a class "AAA" job. Service was congenial and immediate. The food was fine and smoothly served.

Any employee can have an off-day. Everyone knows that. However, the proper application of the soft stuff should ensure the appropriate behavior results–even in moments of crisis.

In my eyes, the airline lost substantial face that day– and I was not alone. Thousands, if not millions, of dollars in advertising couldn't convince me the airline truly believed in customer service. Thus, although no immediate revenue was lost, future revenues were nevertheless put at risk.

Like the case of the misguided security guard, there are, of course, many ways in which the situation could have been handled better. First, the flight attendant could have apologized. Nothing can help a customer feel more as though he is respected than a heartfelt, "I'm sorry. We goofed." The employee could have retrieved the suit bag. Cabin attendants regularly receive deferential treatment by passengers when they walk up and down the aisles. Even if the attendant had to follow behind all other passengers when she did retrieve his suit bag, at least the customer would have felt she was addressing his concerns. Finally, having delivered the bag to the customer, the attendant could have apologized again for the inconvenience.

Hindsight, of course, is 20/20. But, better organizations do train their members in the art of appropriate action during moments of crisis.

The ability to handle emotionally explosive moments, for which no immediate answer exists in any training manual, can be the separator between good organizations and great ones. For the organization to be effective, the individual must address the needs of the customer–at the very moment the incident occurs. Training can help, but codes of behavior become a significant addition, assisting employees when no immediate answer is apparent. So, once a code of behavior is developed, it is the organization's responsibility to train their employees to realize their behavior must reflect that code. Thus, if the organization's code of behavior included "to show every day in every way that we care about our customers," then at the very least, the guard and the attendant would have dealt with their customer more genially and respectfully.

Practising the soft stuff through behavior

I'd bet $50 that the organizations for which the flight attendant and the security guard worked either did not know their purpose, vision or focus, or that they hadn't adequately taken care of the soft stuff needed to deliver it. That may seem like a huge extrapolation from two apparently small incidents, but I believe both situations are revealing.

I believe these two stories show individual behavior–not technology, strategic planning, product superiority, or marketing–most directly affects organizational bottom lines. Again, individual behavior most directly affects organizational bottom lines.

Treating the symptom and not the cause

Employee behavior and, more specifically, employee worth, come into direct question during other organizational crisis points–especially economic ones. Such a point is a recession.

It disturbs me when I hear of organizations "downsizing" and "right-sizing" during recessions. Organizations that reduce payroll in an attempt to cut costs may also be reducing the potential for increasing revenues. People deliver products and services. People make or break an organization. Properly trained employees are not liabilities to be instantly erased from the ledger when things don't "balance." They are assets to be hired, trained, retained and responsibly focused to achieve the required results.

> *In the airline business you find the asset side of the balance sheet is still written in terms of so many aircraft at a value of so many billion dollars. But the real value and test for an airline (service organization) is how many satisfied customers and how many satisfied employees did it end up with during the year? These are the ingredients the airline needs for the future: the customer who is prepared to fly again with the airline next year and the employee who is prepared to perform as well next year.*[10]
>
> JAN CARLZON
> CEO, The SAS Group

Organizations in industries susceptible to world market price fluctuations, like energy, computers, airlines, and agriculture should hire staff very judiciously. Once hired, these individuals should be trained in a way that makes them so valuable to the bottom line that the organization cannot afford to lay them off. If this strikes you as idealistic, then so be it, but perhaps we need to re-think some of our conventional operating methods. Clearly, the present ones aren't working. If you disagree, I challenge you to discuss it with anyone you know who has been laid off.

THE NON-COMMUNICATIVE LEADER

In addition to inadequate training programs and a sometimes skewed organizational view of an individual's worth, a second source of improper organizational behavior is inadequate leadership.

One day, a friend of mine met with a senior manager with whom he was working as a team building consultant. One of the senior manager's colleagues, a middle manager named Fred, had been promoted three months earlier to a new position. My friend asked about Fred.

The senior manager looked distressed. He said he was disappointed with Fred's progress. Fred was not living up to expectations–he seemed to lack direction. Senior management was having second thoughts about him.

My friend asked what management's expectations were of Fred. The senior manager listed three things.

Later that week, my friend met with Fred. Fred explained that he didn't know what direction management wanted him to take. He was extremely frustrated and couldn't figure out how to resolve the problem. Fred was considering looking for another job.

The consultant told Fred that he had met with Fred's boss and that the senior manager had three expectations of him. He told Fred what they were.

Some weeks later, the consultant again met with Fred's manager. He asked how Fred was doing. The senior manager spoke of Fred's sudden "turnaround" in glowing terms. Part way through his description, he paused and asked the consultant if he had spoken to Fred. "Yes," the consultant said. "I told him the three things you expected of him."

He leaned forward, pointed his finger at the consultant and said: "I knew he was cheating!"

Hands-on

There are ways of improving the communication of organizational codes of behavior to individuals and employees in order to avoid these kinds of problems.

Here are a number of questions to get you thinking about improvement if improvement is needed.

■ **What expectations does your leader have of you? Describe two specific behaviors (actions or activities) and the desired results.**

_____

_____

■ **What expectations do you have of your leader? Again, describe two specific behaviors and desired results.**

_____

_____

■ **How will you communicate these expectations to your leader?**

_____

_____

_____

_____

■ What expectations do you have of yourself in your organization? Be specific.

_____

_____

_____

_____

■ Have you communicated your expectations of yourself to your leader? If not, how will you do so?

_____

_____

_____

■ What specific expectations do you have of one of the people whom you supervise (supervising includes parenting)? Choose one person.

Individual's name | _____ |

_____

_____

_____

_____

_____

■ Have you communicated your expectations to the individual mentioned above? If not, how will you do so?

_____

_____

_____

_____

■ What expectations do those you supervise have of you? Be specific.

_____

_____

_____

_____

_____

■ If those you supervise have not communicated their expectations of you, how could you encourage them to do so?

_____

_____

_____

_____

_____

■ **Have you asked those you supervise to develop a list of their expectations of themselves? If not, why not? If you have, what were the results?**

_____

_____

_____

_____

_____

The importance of a code of behavior

Our code of behavior is very significant. First, at the specific level, it helps us identify the actions we need to take to achieve the results we want. Second, at the general level, it provides us with a set of principles. It does not tell us what to do; it tells us *how* to do things.

What we do is not nearly as important as *how* we do it. The security guard was gruff and curt. What he did may have been "right," but *how* he did it was wrong. Similarly, in emptying a crowded closet the flight attendant may have done the "right" thing, but *how* she handled the passenger was wrong. Thus, *it's more important to do things right than to do the right things.* "Doing things right" involves more than just bottom-line results. It keeps us on track towards delivering those bottom lines.

We all know of organizations struggling to survive. Part of their struggle is determining where they must to go to succeed (purpose, vision and focus). The other half is understanding how they're going to get there (the soft stuff and a code of behavior). Then, they have to get moving.

By revisiting your organizational code of behavior on a regular basis, particularly during moments of decision, it should help you emphasize quality first and quantity second. That's doing things right and doing the right things.

In the simplest sense, a code of behavior is a checklist for decision-making. It is also a checklist for acting on those decisions. It can guide us towards organizational "ultimates." It keeps leaders honest, on target and on track. And it enables us to quickly determine whether our decisions are well-founded–not just in the financial short term–but in the long-term well-being of the organization and the world around us.

Changing organizational behaviors won't be easy. Over the ages, organizations have developed innumerable defence mechanisms to fight change. Although these mechanisms sometimes keep negative influences out, more often than not, they also prevent positive influences from getting in. **Be ready for the 50 reasons why something "can't" be changed:**

1. We've never done it before.
2. Nobody else has ever done it before.
3. It has never been tried before.
4. We tried it before.
5. We've been doing it this way for 25 years.
6. It won't work in a small company.
7. It won't work in a large company.
8. It won't work in our company.
9. Why change–it's working okay.
10. The boss will never buy it.
11. It needs further investigation.
12. Our competitors aren't doing it.
13. It's too much trouble to change.
14. Our company is different.
15. The ad department says it can't be sold.
16. Production says it's a bad idea.

17. The service department won't like it.
18. The janitor says it can't be done.
19. It can't be done.
20. We don't have the money.
21. We don't have the personnel.
22. We don't have the equipment.
23. The union will scream.
24. It's too visionary.
25. You can't teach an old dog new tricks.
26. It's too radical a change.
27. It's beyond my responsibility.
28. It's not my job.
29. Don't rock the boat (if you know what's good for you).
30. We don't have the time.
31. It will make other procedures obsolete.
32. Customers won't buy it.
33. It's contrary to policy.
34. It will increase overhead.
35. The employees will never buy it.
36. It's not our problem.
37. I don't like it.
38. You're right but...
39. We're not ready for it.
40. It needs more thought.
41. Management won't accept it.
42. We can't take the chance.
43. We'd lose money on it.
44. It takes too long to pay out.
45. We're doing alright as it is.
46. It needs study by a committee.
47. The competition won't like it.
48. It needs sleeping on.
49. It won't work in this department.
50. It's impossible.

AMERICAN BUSINESS AXIOMS

Here are a few of my personal favorites:

51. Right or wrong, that's the decision we've made, and we're going to stick to it.
52. If you do it, everyone will want to.
53. Who do you think you are?
54. Don't you know the rules around here?
55. The stock market won't like it.
56. Don't do anything without management's approval.

Here's room for some of your own (space may not be sufficient).

57. _____

58. _____

59. _____

60. _____

61. _____

62. _____

63. _____

64. _____

Excuses be damned. Ineffective behavior that is repeated is no more productive than effective behavior that is never tried. If you want to change the behavior of an organization for the better, it will take time–and there will be resistance. Resist the resistance. If you do, the bottom line will prove you right.

FOOTPRINT SIX

The Bottom Line

Success is getting what you want;
happiness is wanting what you get.

ANONYMOUS

You can use most any measure when you're speaking of success.
You can measure it in a fancy home, expensive car or dress.
But the measure of your real success is one you cannot spend
It's the way your child describes you when talking to a friend.

MARTIN BAXBAUM

The buck starts here

The world is obsessed with it; the planet possessed by it. It drives the globe's economies, pushes people to polarities they could not imagine and delivers a generation of dreamers into the unknown. It is money.

The bottom line for millions of individuals worldwide is the balance between income and expenses, assets and liabilities. Success for many in the West is intrinsically linked to financial and material well-being: organizationally it is our profits; individually it is our income. We are taught, however inaccurately, there is only one worthy measure of achievement: the number below the line. "The Western Dream" has become the dream of money, power and possessions.

The game of life

Concentrating only on the bottom line is like focusing solely on the score in a game. It gives us an idea of where things stand, but it offers an extremely narrow view of what is really happening on the field. Suddenly, the players–the ones who actually contribute to the bottom line–fall from sight. If

265

the score indicates a loss, the players can fall from grace. They can be booed, put down in the press, traded or "released." On an individual level, the tragedy can be exasperating. Faced with increasing social pressures, financial insecurity and salaries which do not keep up with the cost of living, the socio-economic climate builds frustration and kills motivation. The coveted luxuries of personal popularity and status, fast cars, swimming pools and dream homes are increasingly out of reach. Yet even those who are fortunate enough to achieve these trappings of "success" are often left with an empty feeling and the nagging question: "Is that all there is?" Based on society's conventional measures of success, this has led some to believe they have come up short.

> *You don't die in North America, you underachieve.*
>
> JERZY KOSINSKI
> American author

Redefining success

> *The secret of happiness is not in doing what one likes, but in liking what one does.*
>
> JAMES MATTHEW BARRIE
> Scottish novelist, dramatist

There is more to life than money. More importantly, there are more measures of success. On our journey through life, we can be honest or dishonest, cruel or kind, vigorous or lazy, courageous or cowardly. These are values, although it is sometimes sad that society does not seem to put much value on them. Television commercials and magazine and newspaper advertising generally paint a picture of personal success based on the lifestyle we live, the car we drive, the company

266

we keep (or run) and the house in which we live. Some are fixated on these signs of "success," and they can truly be a trap. An expensive car is "worth" something to be sure, but it's not worth much if the rest of your life is in ruins. Success is relative, and relatively nebulous–until we define it for ourselves.

Defining success

When we die, we are not remembered for how much money we made, but for how we lived–for our values and for our principles. It is as if the real measuring stick of our contribution as human beings isn't determined until the innings are out, we've left the game and the crowd gets a chance to reassess the score. The key to living a truly successful life is to never lose sight of what's really important. Or, perhaps more importantly, we must know what *really isn't* important.

Quality versus quantity

We in the West love measures–measures of wealth, status and power. Large portions of the entire infrastructure of our society–everything from advertising to marketing are based on them. But when we're faced with journeys that cannot easily be quantified–our lives–we can run into trouble. Often, we try to apply the same old scales of money, material wealth and lifestyle. The problem is, most of the old scales don't apply anymore in any meaningful way. We need new measures–measures that are more oriented towards our less quantifiable destinations–our human ones.

A more accurate measure of success besides money might be our contribution to the lives of others, our personal sense of self-satisfaction and our level of self-esteem. These are better measures, I believe, because they are internal. And, they are determined by each individual.

What success isn't

As we travel through our forest of life, we soon discover there is no one destination that will bring us total fulfilment. After reaching one destination, we must soon decide on our next goals. Then, we must set out for them.

The first step in measuring our greatness is to know what success is–or just as importantly, what it is not.

Success isn't simple to achieve, but it is simple to understand–it's what **you** say it is. It's not what society says it is, or the guy next door, or your best friend, or even your spouse or significant other. It's not what TV says it is, or magazines, or newspapers or even this book. I repeat: **success is what you say it is**. Period. There is no other measure–no other meaningful measure anyway.

> The easiest thing to be in the world is you. The most difficult thing to be is what other people want you to be. Don't let them put you in that position.
>
> LEO BUSCAGLIA
> American educator
> and author

Before we talk about your definition of success, let's consider two larger concepts. The first I call "The Balance of Your Life." The second is "The Everest Effort." These may provide you with a larger framework in which to consider your success.

The balance of your life

The most frequently asked question I get as a consultant is: "How do I live a balanced life?"

A professor I had in graduate school offered one answer. During the final class of the term, instead of wrapping up the course as we all expected, he proceeded to wrap up life– and how to live it.

He started by drawing three circles on the board. Inside the first circle he wrote, "Work"; in the second he wrote, "Personal/Self"; and in the third, "Family."

In the space provided below, draw three circles. Label one for work, one for personal/self and one for family. Choose a "typical" week and adjust the size of each circle according to how much time you've spent in each of these three areas over the last seven days. Thus, if you typically spend more time on work than on your family, make the size of your work circle bigger. If you spend more time on yourself than on your family, make that circle bigger.

Take a minute to draw your circles here:

The sizes of your circles

Chances are, the sizes of your circles are all different. That's because we don't have much balance in our lives. Imbalance is okay for a short time, but it can be disastrous if it keeps up for long periods.

I recognize there are moments in our lives when we consciously come out of balance. As I mentioned in Footprint 1, during tax time, millions of accountants throw themselves totally into their work. That's perfectly acceptable as long as the imbalance is corrected when the deadline has passed. **Balance is not a point in time. It must be measured over time.**

Your life, and the components of it, are like trees in a forest. They all have their own circles of space. If the circle of shade created by a single tree (one area of your life) gets too large, the other trees around it will not get enough sunlight. As a result, they will suffer. Some may wither and die.

In nature, this is "survival of the fittest." But in an individual, what dies isn't the competition. It is a part of us. Since all areas of our life can be vital, we cannot afford to neglect any of them.

The appearance of your circles

Chances are equally good that your circles are not overlapping. That's because we have a tendency to compartmentalize our lives. Some people believe one aspect of their lives does not affect other aspects. In fact, they are all linked together–like a set of Olympic rings. Because of this, weakness in one eventually affects the others.

The first circle–work

I can still remember what my professor said about the three circles. He explained that for many of us, work would become the centre of our lives. Careers demanded at least eight hours a day, five days a week. If we wanted to be upwardly mobile, he said, we'd probably have to work 12-to-14-hour days, six and even seven days a week. But our jobs, he cautioned, must not be allowed to overcome our lives.

When I heard that, I said to myself, "Not this cowboy!" It couldn't happen to me.

Within just a few months of graduation, however, the symptoms of workaholism were showing in me. Soon, I was working seven days a week. It almost cost me my family and my health. Thus, my professor was something of a prophet in addition to being a first-class educator.

> *Organizational alignment is seen by its advocates as different from the situation where an individual sacrifices his or her own identity to the organization. It is rather the expansion of the individual's identity and sense of purpose to include the organization and its purpose. I believe, however, that there is a shadow side to the benefits....The idea that we can achieve perfect integration between the needs of the people and the purposes of the organization is fatally flawed.* [1]
>
> RICHARD HARRISON
> Author

With the above warning in mind let's see how we can escape being "captured" by our environment–organizational or otherwise.

The second circle–personal/self

My professor described the second circle, personal/self, as taking time to regenerate yourself in a physical and psychological way. Good physical health, he said, is usually coupled with good mental health. Without good physical and mental health, he explained, it is difficult to be effective in our work or with our family. Some special people succeed in spite of failing physical health, but not without extraordinary effort, dogged determination and high self-esteem.

271

So, how does one look after personal/self? One way to look after yourself is by taking proper vacations. That's not news to anyone. How you take vacations may be.

The time-off trick

When I first entered the work force, I thought my job was too important to leave for an extended time. So, rather than take all my holidays at once, I played a "smart" little trick. I stretched out my vacation time. Instead of taking ten days off at once, I'd take a day a week for ten weeks.

The trick was on me. My productivity at work dropped dramatically. First, I was never fully rested–I never fully unplugged. Second, I never managed to take all the time off I said I would. Little "emergencies" always kept me from taking even one day off during the week.

Since then, I have discovered that to take full advantage of holidays, you have to take them in long enough blocks of time. In the first week of a three-week holiday, for example, psychologically you're still back at the office. During the second week, you begin to move away from work and start appreciating your surroundings. By the third week, you have transferred your focus to your surroundings.

The third week is the whole reason for the holiday. But like anything worthwhile, you have to invest something to achieve it. In this case, you invest time–and probably money too.

If you handle your holiday properly, the return on your investment should be much greater than the three weeks. A good holiday should enable you to handle the stress of work for many weeks after your return.

Well-planned and restful holidays are also excellent ways for family to rejuvenate itself. If you return from your vacation exhausted, which many individuals and families do, a large part of the holiday's purpose is not achieved. If you want to "cut loose" and have a wild time, that's fine. But

272

if you're under a lot of stress, relaxation and mild exercise may be what's most needed. Packing too much into a holiday can be just as stressful as trying to pack too much into a day at work.

It's important to know the purpose of your holiday. You may visualize yourself lying on the beach (vision) and focus on relaxing. Your soft stuff may include everything from a peaceful mental attitude to suntan oil, sunglasses and an intriguing novel. Your code of behavior may include a stubborn insistence on not getting caught up in anything except nothing. Your vacation plan may be to have no plan–and to stick to it.

Rules for longevity:

- *Avoid fried meats which angry up the blood.*

- *If your stomach disputes you, lie down and pacify it with cool thoughts.*

- *Keep the juices flowing by jangling around gently as you move.*

- *Go very light on the vices, such as carrying on in society. The social ramble ain't restful.*

- *Avoid running at all times.*

- *Don't look back. Something might be gaining on you.*

> LEROY "SATCHEL" PAIGE
> American baseball player

The third circle–family

Our family, my professor said, is the most important of the three circles. Without a good family life, whether in the present, past or future, it will be difficult for you to do your best in any facet of your life. Your health, particularly your mental and emotional health, will also suffer.

In the western world, the family usually takes third place behind work and self. You don't get paid to do it, it doesn't improve your social or professional status, and your performance within it is virtually invisible to most outsiders.

While the rewards of a happy family life may not earn you salary increases, they can bring you joy that is lasting and genuine. Salaries can be taken away, bonuses can be withdrawn and you can be laid off, transferred, demoted or fired. But the joy in your mate's or child's eyes when you help make them happier can never be taken away. It is priceless because it is the ultimate reflection of you as a person, not as a professional, a manager, a colleague or a leader. Titles don't count in families. There, you are judged solely on *you*.

To plan the success of a family or a relationship takes as much effort as does a career. Sometimes we think they will take care of themselves. They don't.

Like anything worthwhile, relationships must be nurtured. People often grow apart in families because they don't organize themselves like they organize their careers. Somehow, there seems to be less at stake.

In fact, more is at stake. Ask anyone who has lost a relationship that meant a lot to them. Good jobs can be replaced. Good partners are more difficult to find.

The fourth circle

Over the years, I have taken to adding a fourth circle to the three rings: *"spirituality."*

Some people get uncomfortable when you talk about spiritual issues. For them, this dimension doesn't exist. If that is how you feel, then you may wish to stand by it.

The spiritual dimension of our lives surfaces when we pause in wonder at an event not readily explicable in the "real" world. There might be a sense of magic in the air, or we might feel deeply touched by something.

The birth of my children was a spiritual event for me. It made me step back and ask, "Why?" Why are we here on Earth? Why am I here and what should I do with my life? Are we all here by accident or is there some greater presence we should try to get in touch with?

If there is one theme that runs through humankind and separates us from the rest of the animal kingdom, it is the continuing search for personal meaning. Primitive peoples, remote island cultures and complex urban societies all have one thing in common–the search for something or someone greater than themselves.

Over the centuries, humankind has designed elaborate ceremonies in an attempt to communicate directly with some spiritual realm. Many believe there is a power somewhere that can make a negative and/or positive difference in their lives. They, therefore, choose to worship.

Questions in crises

I find it interesting that people often turn to worship in times of personal crises. The importance of religion increases in times of hardship and diminishes in times of plenty. I wonder why we have to get to the point of despair before we begin to develop our spirituality.

I once heard a story that vividly impressed this point on me. While it has obvious religious implications, the story can be read on many levels.

God and the Devil were competing for peoples' hearts and souls. The Devil was given free reign to try to win over humankind. He tried starvation, suffering, pestilence, disease–any disaster he could think of. Nothing worked. The people remained true to God.

God said: "You see, Devil, there is nothing you can do to turn the people from me."

Suddenly, the Devil had a brilliant idea. He retorted: "But there is something I can do! I will give them everything they want–jewels, fast horses, the finest food, the nicest clothes, the biggest homes and the most money."

The outcome was a windfall for Mr. Lucifer.

I'm not saying material wealth is bad. It isn't. It drives our western economies. I know that. I also know I enjoy having money as much as the next person. But we must not become possessed by our possessions. As I have said before, the more we think we have it made, the more unconsciously incompetent we become.

The 365-day split

A friend of mine gave me a useful guide to attaining balance in life. He had a very successful career as an advertising agency executive. As his career was winding down, he realized he had placed too much importance on his professional work. So, in his early 60s, he set himself a new goal. He took the 365 days in a year and re-allocated them to the four facets of his life: 100 days for his work; 100 days for his family; 100 days for himself; and 65 days for his spiritual journey. It is too soon to tell you the outcome of his actions, but I can say he appears to be a more satisfied man.

Your circles revisited

With the above points in mind, draw the three (or four) circles to which you aspire below. Your objective should be to attain a balance during the next four weeks. This does not mean you should attain it 30 days from now. It means that during the next month, you should try to make the changes necessary to ultimately achieve this balance. The difference is subtle, but important. It is journey, not destination, oriented.

Draw your circles here:

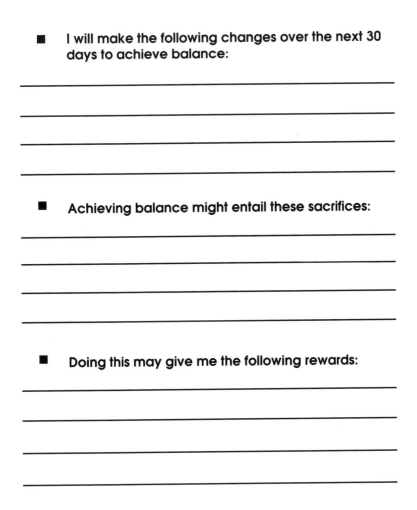

- **I will make the following changes over the next 30 days to achieve balance:**

_____

_____

_____

_____

- **Achieving balance might entail these sacrifices:**

_____

_____

_____

_____

- **Doing this may give me the following rewards:**

_____

_____

_____

_____

A look back

Your circles should be revisited during your time-outs for time-ins (see Footstep 4). Like all aspects of your purpose, vision, focus, soft stuff and code of behavior, they are worth reviewing periodically to see if you are staying on course to your goal. So:

The dates of my quarterly "Balance of Life" reviews over the next two years will be: (dd/mm/yy). Use as many as you need, or add more if you wish.

	DAY	MONTH	YEAR
Balance of Life Review 1:			
Balance of Life Review 2:			
Balance of Life Review 3:			
Balance of Life Review 4:			
Balance of Life Review 5:			
Balance of Life Review 6:			
Balance of Life Review 7:			
Balance of Life Review 8:			
Balance of Life Review 9:			
Balance of Life Review 10:			

To ensure they are not forgotten, you might wish to enter these dates on a calendar or in your day book. Do this now.

One U.S. businessman has a novel view of life, work and personal balance. In response to a November 30, 1992, *Fortune* magazine article, "Welcome to the Age of Overwork," he wrote the following letter to the editor:

> I will fire anyone in my company who habitually spends more than 50 hours a week in the office–for three reasons: First, an employee who's not strongly connected to what's going on outside the office doesn't understand our customers. Second, an employee who doesn't keep his or her social life–friends, lovers, spouse, children, relatives– has atrophying social skills and makes a poor team player. Third, an employee who willingly overworks himself or herself doesn't have the get-up-and-go to correct inefficiency and is keeping the company down.[2]
>
> TOM U. GARDNER
> Boston, Mass.

The excellence in effort

> Notice the difference between what happens when a man says to himself, 'I have failed three times,' and what happens when he says, 'I am a failure.'
>
> S.I. HAYAKAWA
> U.S. senator, semanticist

Besides balance, there is at least one other important factor to consider when measuring success. That factor is effort.

I believe if our efforts are absolute, if we put 100 per cent into our goals, regardless of whether we actually achieve those goals, we will come away satisfied.

279

Alan Hobson, whom we've mentioned previously, and his colleague, Jamie Clarke, call this "The Everest Effort." They went to Mount Everest in the autumn of 1991 as part of an expedition to the northern, Chinese side of the mountain. Their team faced extremely uncooperative weather. The expedition nearly lost three members when the trio got stuck out in an horrific storm at 25,000 feet. No one from any country had ever reached the top of Everest from the north side at that time and the route they were attempting has never yet been used on a successful ascent in the autumn climbing season.

Alan returned home to respond to allegations that his team had failed. His response was revealing–and enlightening. "We did not fail," he said proudly. "We gave it absolutely everything we had–almost our lives. When we go back next time (spring 1994), we will do some things differently. This time, though, we made an Everest Effort. In the words of Gandhi, 'Total Effort is Total Victory.'

> *There is no such thing as failure except to those who accept and believe in failure.*
>
> ORISON SWETT MARDEN
> American lawyer

It may sound like a rationalization to say: **"It's not whether you win or lose. It's how you play the game,"** but there is great wisdom in this idea. That wisdom has far more to do with the eventual outcome of effort than it does with the ethics of how a game was played.

To explain: If we put 100 per cent into everything we do, and we keep doing it day in and day out, eventually, we will succeed–provided we make the proper effort.

Another important factor to consider when we're talking about effort is the relative nature of the term. To progress from a mark of "D" in reading to a "C," will likely require far more effort for a learning-disabled student than for an unchallenged person. Thus another important component in the measurement of success is the degree of improvement, especially given the skill set of the individual. **Success can only be measured within ourselves, by ourselves.** If we continually judge our progress by comparing ourselves to others, we will always be disappointed because there will always be someone better than us.

> *God grant me the serenity to accept the things I cannot change, courage to change the things I can, and the wisdom to know the difference.*
>
> attributed to RHEINHOLD NIEBUHR
> American theologian
> used as a prayer
> (by Alcoholics Anonymous)

Ignoring outcomes

Forget about outcomes for a moment. Write down those areas in your life in which you are making the biggest effort. Beside each, rate your effort by an indicator of 1 to 10. If you're busting your backside with as much intelligence, initiative, guts and gusto as you can muster, give yourself a 10. If you're close to that ideal, give yourself a 9; very close, an 8; getting there, a 7; aspiring to it, a 6; halfway there, a 5; and so on.

It might be useful to add a third column to the chart– one for "Quality of Effort." In this column, on a scale of 1 to 10, rate the intelligence of your efforts. In other words, is your effort effective? Is it well thought out? There's no sense in putting out 100 per cent doing something incorrectly. It won't work any more in life than it will in bicycle riding.

	Activity	Effort indicator	Quality of effort
1.			
2.			
3.			
4.			
5.			

From evaluation of effort to action

Once you measure your effort in each category, you can determine an action plan to either maintain or improve your efforts. So...

1.   Activity _____

   Action needed to maintain my effort

   _____

   _____

   Action needed to improve my effort

   _____

   _____

2.   Activity _____

   Action needed to maintain my effort

   _____

   _____

Action needed to improve my effort

_____

_____

3.   **Activity** _____

      Action needed to maintain my effort

_____

_____

      Action needed to improve my effort

_____

_____

4.   **Activity** _____

      Action needed to maintain my effort

_____

_____

      Action needed to improve my effort

_____

_____

5.   **Activity** _____

      Action needed to maintain my effort

_____

_____

      Action needed to improve my effort

_____

_____

*It is not the critic who counts, not the man
who points out how the strong man stumbled,
or where the doer of deeds could have done
them better. The credit belongs to the man
who is actually in the arena; whose face is
marred by dust and sweat and blood; who
strives valiantly; who errs and who comes up
short again and again; who knows the great
enthusiasms, the great devotions, and spends
himself in a worthy cause; who, at best, knows
in the end the triumph of high achievement;
and who, at worst, at least fails while daring
greatly, so that his place shall never be with
those cold and timid souls who know neither
victory nor defeat.*

THEODORE ROOSEVELT
26th president of the United States

Arriving at your bottom line

*The darkest hour of any man's life is when
he sits down to plan how to get money
without earning it.*

HORACE GREELEY
American journalist, politician

Have you ever heard of someone who has won a lottery–and
then lost at life? Frequently, the effects of a huge windfall
create such stress in the winners that their lives fall apart. By
all outward indications, they have "arrived." Yet so many of
them seem to depart into a huge hole just as soon as they get
"there." The question is–why? Why would someone who has
just "made it" suddenly "break it"?

284

The answer, I believe, is they arrived at the destination without taking the journey. If they'd made the journey, they would have arrived with an appreciation of the effort needed and become better stewards of their new found wealth. Similarly, when parents provide their children with everything, they are actually doing them a disservice. They are in effect handing them the winning lottery ticket. There's no effort required.

The lottery (or lack) of life

The real world, of course, doesn't work like a lottery. There's far less chance in it, at least far less than some believe. Yes, luck does enter into life, sometimes prominently.

> *Luck is a dividend of sweat. The more you sweat, the luckier you get.*
>
> RAY KROC
> Founder,
> McDonald's Corporation

I believe we are largely masters of our own destiny. Yes, there are elements outside our control, but the majority are within our control.

The bottom line on your bottom line

To keep on track it is important to review your purpose, vision, focus, soft stuff and code of behavior occasionally. You may find yourself asking: "Is that all there is to determining my bottom lines?" "All I have to do is review Footprints 1 through 5?" The answer is yes.

285

That's the way it's supposed to be. Unfortunately, it's not the way it usually is in life. Usually, we put all the emphasis on the bottom line, not on what happens above the bottom line. But if we put the emphasis on the process and not the outcome, the outcome will take care of itself.

Your bottom line is attainable if you've done all the previous steps properly. This sequence of "effort first" and "outcome second" holds in almost any endeavour–whether it is running a relationship, raising a family or just making it through the day. For example, for a writer who has brought a story word by word into the world, when the work finally comes out in print, it can be a little anticlimactic. That is usually not the public's perception, but it is often the author's. Similarly, when an Olympic gold medallist steps onto the top of the podium, what goes through their mind is usually what it took to stand there. That's why so many of them cry. They are overwhelmed by the magnitude of the effort–and the sudden acclaim. The performer feels the mountain, but the public sees the peak.

Regardless of your position–student, business person, homemaker, sales executive, government employee or charity fund-raiser–you are the performer. So, measure your steps as you take them, not as you end them.

And now, here's the news...

I've got good news and bad news. The good news is you've reached the last part of the last Footprint. The bad news is you're still in the woods–and always will be.

> *Once you get into this great stream of history, you can't get out.*

> RICHARD M. NIXON
> 37th president of the
> United States

This isn't a cover-up. This book is a Six-Step Guide. There is a first step and there is a sixth step. The rub, however, is the sixth step is not the last step. In fact there is no last step. The process is a continuous one–circular and repetitive.

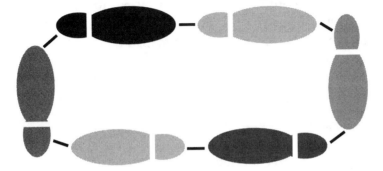

This book really has no beginning and no end. Like the programs in "The Soft Stuff," it isn't a step-by-step procedure at all. It describes a process. Processes, as you will recall from Footprint 4, are ongoing.

> *Failure is never final and success is never ending.*
> *Success is a journey, not a destination.*
>
> DR. ROBERT SCHULLER
> American evangelist

The woods never really end until we die. After that, heaven knows what happens. But regardless of how near we are to the end of our trail, we still need some means of measuring our journey–some bottom lines. Every few miles or so, we need to know how we're doing. Without it, we have no way of knowing if we've arrived, or if we're still travelling.

In the strictest sense, as I explained, we don't want to "arrive." The moment we "arrive" is the moment we depart. Complacency breeds contentment, and contentment can breed complacency. By now, your pack should contain many of the tools necessary to improve your personal life in a positive and dynamic way.

You should know why you're on your trail (purpose); who you'd ultimately like to be when you reach your destination (vision); what you'll need to concentrate on to get there (focus); what you'll need to have and know to get there (the soft stuff); and how you'll need to act en route (behavior). If you've done all of those things properly, the results (bottom lines) should happen naturally.

Your personal journey should now have a disciplined, effective and exciting approach. You have embarked on a great adventure. Bon voyage!

> People are unreasonable, illogical and
> self-centered.
> **Love them anyway.**
> If you do good, people will accuse you of
> selfish ulterior motives.
> **Do good anyway.**
> If you are successful, you will win false
> friends and true enemies.
> **Succeed anyway.**
> Honesty and frankness make you vulnerable.
> **Be honest and frank anyway.**
> The good you do today will be forgotten tomorrow.
> **Do good anyway.**
> The biggest people with the biggest ideas can
> be shot down by the smallest people with the
> smallest minds.
> **Think big anyway.**
> People favor underdogs but always follow top
> dogs.
> **Fight for some underdogs anyway.**
> What you spend years building may be destroyed
> overnight.
> **Build anyway.**
> Give the world the best you've got and you'll be
> kicked in the teeth.
> **Give the world the best you've got anyway.**
>
> DR. ROBERT SCHULLER
> American evangelist

FOOTPRINT SIX

The Bottom Line

Part II : Organizational

*To change and to improve are two
different things.*

GERMAN PROVERB

The final test of a leader is that he leaves behind in other people the convictions and the will to carry on.

WALTER LIPPMANN
American author

On an organizational level, **"success"** is thought to be easy to measure. In corporations, it's things such as profits, return on investment, earnings per share, dividends to shareholders and growth. In non-profit or governmental organizations, it's the size of the department, the number of employees or the size of the budget. Of late, it's the size of the deficit. In families, success can be the size of the family home or the number of cars in the driveway. These measures can become an obsession for some organizations.

There is another dimension to organizational success besides numbers, dollars, shares, budgets or cars. Surprisingly, it is identical to the one we talked about in the footprint on individual bottom line–what is the legacy left behind? What is the organization's footprint–its lasting impression not only on the world, but on the people who work within it?

An organization's bottom line has more to do with employee behavior than with financial statements. The sooner we get ourselves programmed away from numbers and towards people, the sooner we'll start to realize the potential profits–financial and otherwise.

Organizational bottom lines, as I see them, encompass far more than the financial statements. That's why in this footprint, we'll be concentrating on something other than the financials. I'd like to focus on performance appraisal systems. The reason for this is simple and I've said it many times already–people, not products, produce profits. If your people are producing for you, they'll produce profits for you. I liken it to an engine. If you want to increase the speed of a car,

290

there's no use in just clocking it on a track. You must look under the hood and figure out how you can improve what's driving it–the pistons.

This brings us to the beginning of the end of our journey through this book. You may find this last Footprint a bit anticlimactic. It's supposed to be! As I mentioned, if you take all the previous steps properly, the bottom lines should take care of themselves. Essentially, all we're going to do in this Footprint is review Footprints one through five. That's all there is to bottom lines–if you've made the previous five Footprints properly.

Performance appraisal systems

Performance appraisal systems direct the efforts of people towards organizational purpose, vision and focus. They also bring the soft stuff to life and determine whether your organizational code of behavior is being adhered to. I'd like to start, as usual, with a few important questions:

- ■ **How do you measure the performance of the people within your organization? In other words, what is your current system of individual performance appraisal?**

_____

_____

_____

_____

_____

■   What are the specific individual activities that move your organization towards its bottom lines? If you're in a family, it might be the number of family meals you have together or the recreational activities you share each week. If you're in a sales organization, it might be the number of sales calls each sales person makes in a day. In manufacturing, it might be the number of error-free parts you produce per hour.

Activities

_____

_____

_____

_____

_____

_____

_____

■   Do you and the members of your organization look forward to performance appraisals? Why or why not?

_____

_____

_____

If you can answer the questions above with confidence and in a positive manner, then you are well on your way to developing your bottom lines.

If you're like most employees of organizations, however, the answer to 1 will be sketchy, the answer to 2 will be non-existent, and the answer to 3 will be a definite "no."

Bursting the bubble

I once experienced the double-edged sword of performance appraisal as an employee with a major educational institution. I was fortunate enough to attain one of the highest performance scores for my year's work. But my bubble was burst by a single line in the comment section of the appraisal form. There, my superior made a negative statement about my loyalty to the organization. I was devastated. I was furious not only because I felt the statement was inaccurate, but also because of my supervisor's reaction to my concern. "Don't worry about it," he told me. "You know how 'the boss' is. We always have to say something negative no matter how good the rating is!"

I don't need to tell you how deflating that conversation was. The leader believed he had to keep his employees in line. The only way to do that was to point out negatives, even if those negatives did not hold water.

Anyone who knows anything about behavior modification systems will tell you this kind of negative reinforcement doesn't work. Yet it is alive and well in many organizations today. If you expect to produce positive performance or create a positive culture in yourself or your organization, I don't recommend it.

The same lesson holds true in families. Time and again I hear parents praise their children in private, but criticize them in public. If you want positive results, you have to reward positively–and consistently.

Tough calls

Everyone wants to know where they stand in other people's eyes. Yet few want to risk making a subjective judgment on someone else's performance. Evaluation is an art. Unfortunately, many who conduct performance appraisals continue to try to turn it into a science–a fill-in-the-blanks, enter-the-numbers, push-the-buttons and presto–out comes an airtight measure of the individual.

Few people look forward to personal appraisal sessions. That's because many of the performance systems available today produce vague results. Both managers and employees leave these meetings angry and frustrated. It's no wonder few look forward to the process.

Unfortunately, there is no definitive answer. But, there are better options.

Two good performance appraisal systems

In my travels, I have come across two performance appraisal systems that embody many of the elements needed to transform science into art. They concentrate not only on organizational effectiveness, but also on personal development. Best of all, they're easy to understand.

The Regent College example

Dr. Walter Wright, as you may recall from Footprint 4, organizational soft stuff, is the president of Regent College in Vancouver, Canada. Regent College is one of North America's larger seminaries.

Once a year, Dr. Wright asks employees to fill out a simple review form. It includes questions such as:

■ How do you feel about the last 12 months you've spent with us? Do you feel you are part of the team?

■ Have we fulfilled your expectations of us? Is our role with you adequate in your mind?

■ Your job description–is it accurate given what you have been doing in the past year?

294

- How do you feel you have managed to respond to the issues we have addressed?

- Do we need to set objectives to help resolve issue(s) in the above question?

- What do you want to do in the next 12 months to make your job more interesting?

- Do we see and agree on specific objectives for the next 12 months?

- What can I do this year to help you move towards your goals and provide opportunities to enhance your career?

Regent College's whole system is designed to look at personal development and personal evaluation. Notice how none of the questions ask anything about money or position—bottom lines. While these may well enter the   answers, the questions are directed at the soft stuff above the bottom line. (Salary reviews occur annually and are negotiated with the board of directors. They are usually not a concern because everyone at the same rank is paid the same.)

The questions are answered by employees and then submitted to their managers before an annual discussion. During this session, agreement is reached by both parties. Then the agreement is typed, signed by both parties and filed until the next evaluation. At that time, it is reviewed prior to any other discussions.

Johnsonville Foods Inc.

Another of the more innovative performance appraisal systems I've run across is one used by Johnsonville Foods Inc., of Sheboygan, Wisconsin, a city on the northwestern shore of Lake Michigan.

In an article called "How I Learned to Let My Workers Lead,"[1] Johnsonville Foods CEO, Ralph Stayer, includes the company's "performance-share evaluation form." What's ingenious about the form is that, by looking at it, employees immediately know the three focal points of the organization: **performance, teamwork** and **personal development**. The evaluation is completed every six months.

JOHNSONVILLE FOODS, INC.
COMPANY PERFORMANCE-SHARE
EVALUATION FORM [2]

Please check one: _____ self _____ coach

(Johnsonville doesn't use the terms "employee" and "manager." The organization believes these are too hierarchical.)

1.   PERFORMANCE

A. Customer Satisfaction

How do I rate the quality of the work I do? Do I contribute my best to producing a product to be proud of–one that I would buy or encourage someone else to buy?

Score _____ (1 - 9)

B. Cost Effectiveness

To what extent do I perform my job cost-effectively? Do I strive to work smarter? To work more productively with fewer errors? To complete my job quickly, eliminating overtime when possible? To reduce waste in all departments?

Score _____

C. Attitude

To what extent do I have a positive attitude toward my personal, department and company goals as expressed by my actions, feelings and thoughts? Do I like to come to work? Am I thoughtful and considerate of fellow members? Do I work to promote better attitudes? Do I demonstrate company loyalty?

Score _____

D. Responsibility

To what extent do I take responsibility for my job? Do I accept a challenge? Am I willing to take on or look for additional responsibilities? Do I work independently of supervision?

Score _____

E. Ideas

To what extent have I offered ideas and suggestions for improvements? Do I suggest better ways of doing things instead of just complaining?

Score _____

F. Problem Solver / Preventer

To what extent have I contributed to solving or preventing problems? Do I anticipate problem situations and try to avoid them? Do I push-pull when necessary? Do I keep an open line of communication?

Score _____

G. Safety

To what extent do my actions show my concern for safety for myself and others? Do I alert co-workers to unsafe procedures? Do I alert my coach to unsafe conditions in my department?

Score _____

297

H. Quality Image

To what extent have I displayed a high-quality image in my appearance, language, personal hygiene, and working environment?

Score _____

II.   TEAMWORK

A. Contribution to Groups

How would I rate my contribution to my department's performance? Am I aware of department goals? Do I contribute to a team? Do I communicate with team members?

Score _____

B. Communication

To what extent do I keep others informed to prevent problems from occurring? Do I work to promote communication between plants and departments? Do I relay information to the next shift? Do I speak up at meetings and let my opinions and feelings be known?

Score _____

C. Willingness to Work Together

To what extent am I willing to share the responsibility of getting the work done? Do I voluntarily assist others to obtain results? Do I demonstrate a desire to accomplish department goals? Do I complete paperwork accurately and thoroughly and work toward a smooth flow of information throughout the company? Am I willing to share in any overtime?

Score _____

D. Attendance and Timeliness

Do I contribute to the team by being present and on time for work (including after breaks and lunch)? Do I realize the inconvenience and hardship caused by my absence or tardiness?

Score _____

III. PERSONAL DEVELOPMENT

A. To what extent am I actively involved in lifelong learning? Taking classes is not the only way to learn. Other ways include use of our resource centre or libraries for reading books, articles, etc.

Score _____

B. Do I improve my job performance by applying what I have learned?

Score _____

C. Do I ask questions pertaining to my job and other jobs too?

Score _____

D. Do I try to better myself not only through work but in all aspects of my life?

Score _____

E. Do I seek information about our industry?

Score _____

TOTAL POINTS _____

The primary reason I like this performance appraisal system is that it focuses on what the company wants to achieve–for its customers and for its employees. Second, it is simple to understand and to apply, both for the coach (manager) and employee. Third, it features a scoring system broad enough in scope not to become a science, yet narrow enough to produce the art of open and honest discussion between coach and employee. Fourth, and most important, everyone realizes Johnsonville's system isn't perfect. Participants are periodically unhappy, but generally, most employees are very pleased with it. This is because employees invented this system, implement it and regularly change it to ensure that it is fair and accurate.

Moving from system to solution

As the article goes on to explain, Johnsonville has a novel way of recording and interpreting the data. Average-level scores of three, four or five are recorded on the corresponding line, but lower scores like 1 or 2 and higher scores such as 6, 7, 8 or 9 usually call for some explanation.

Prior to every evaluation session, each employee's coach fills out the same evaluation. Then, both participants talk about all 17 topics. Total points must be within a 9-point spread. If they are, an average of the two totals is taken. This yields a final score. If member and coach cannot get within the 9-point spread, an arbitration group stands ready. As of the date of the article, arbitration had never been required.

Performance appraisal and personal development

Before you evaluate anyone, it's important to know the answer to a key question: Do you want to do performance appraisal or personal development? Performance appraisal measures and comments on an individual's past performance. Personal development improves future performance and evaluates career opportunities.

Ideally, you should do both. However, if an employee gets a poor performance appraisal, he is usually not receptive to improving his performance. Because he is human, his first reaction is often defensive.

There is a three-part solution.

First, develop an expectation in your organization that frequent personal appraisals are a required and routine activity. This will reduce the stress and improve the way appraisals are perceived.

Second, base your performance appraisal system on the specific activities needed to meet your organization's goals. (See Footprints 1 through 5. They establish organizational baselines for expected behavior.) This will prevent the appraisal from getting too personal. People who are criticized personally react instinctively. You want them to react effectively. To achieve this, everyone must know and understand the organization's strategic plan, its purpose, vision, focus, soft stuff and code of behavior.

Third, make your performance appraisal system specific to each part of your organization. Too many systems are developed by a central body that tries to set standards for the entire organization. This can be frustrating for an individual and might elicit a defensive reaction.

A portion of the appraisal system can have central organizational requirements for performance, but most of it should focus on the specific needs and goals of the area in which the individual functions. In a corporation, the needs of the accounting department will be very different from those of the marketing department.

To bring a few of these concepts to life, consider these questions:

- In general, list your organization's expectations of the individuals within it. (This may look similar to the exercise you just completed in Footprint 5–behavior–but its objectives are different.)

Expectations

_____

_____

_____

_____

_____

- List your organizational area's (department, family, whatever) expectations of the individuals within it.

Expectations

_____

_____

_____

_____

_____

■ If you were to create a blend of expectations in which roughly three-quarters of it were to be specific to your area and one-quarter were to pertain to overall organizational expectations, what might the blend look like?

My area (75%):
Expectations

_____

_____

_____

_____

_____

_____

Organizational (25%):
Expectations

_____

_____

_____

■ Which of the above expectations relate to performance appraisal?

_____

_____

_____

_____

■ Which relate to personal development?

_____

_____

_____

_____

_____

■ How could you develop the expectation that frequent personal appraisals be a routine activity in your area?

_____

_____

_____

■ What are the specific activities needed to meet your area's goals?

_____

_____

_____

_____

■ How could you base your performance appraisal system on these areas?

_____

_____

_____

_____

Ready, aim...

The best performance appraisal systems have specific targets and are developed by both leaders and followers. The greater everyone's input from development to implementation, the more positively the appraisal system will be viewed by everyone.

- **If you have a performance appraisal system in your area, how many individuals were involved in its development?**

_____

_____

- **How could you revise your area's current performance appraisal system so it involves a wider cross-section of people?**

_____

_____

_____

_____

Dealing with job descriptions

I believe job descriptions should be less significant in most organizations than they now are. More importance should be placed on performance appraisal systems. While job descriptions tell individuals what the job entails, performance appraisal systems tell them how they're expected to execute the job.

A job description doesn't have a close enough link to the outcome of the desired behavior. **The closer the link between behavior and bottom lines, the better the bottom line will be.**

305

Screening candidates for your organization

Explain your performance appraisal system to prospective members of your organization. This should help prevent confusion between what they expect and what your organization requires. You should also explain your organization's purpose, vision, focus and code of behavior to them. If they are not prepared to live up to the standards of your organization, it is better for them–and you–to discover this before they join.

The bottom line on organizational bottom lines

The Six Steps I have outlined in this book can be applied to almost any process in life. Whether you want to build a home, raise a family or climb the corporate ladder, the process is exactly the same. First, you have to determine where you want to go and, most importantly, why you want to make your journey (purpose). Then you have to decide who you want to be when you get to your destination (vision). This accomplished, you need to figure out what you're going to concentrate on to get there (focus); what physical and psychological equipment you'll need (the soft stuff); and finally, what you'll need to do and how you'll need to do it (behavior).

In summary, let's take two common organizational examples: raising a family and increasing the membership of a local club. As we've dealt with corporate examples throughout this book, I thought we should finish by bringing this whole process into a broader context. The Footprints can be universally applied.

Achievement Challenge 1: Raising a Family

Purpose: Creating a home that will enable family members to make a positive contribution to the world.

Vision: To be a healthy, happy place where family members will feel at home.

Focus: Contributing, nurturing, sanctuary

Soft Stuff

Staple 1: Communicating purpose, vision and focus

Spend time together as a family during holidays, at meal times and make time together for games and recreation.

Staple 2: Training and development

Help one another develop discipline in completing our work assignments and encourage family members to take and complete educational courses that develop individual skills (e.g., computer or fitness training). Take part in family retreats with and without facilitators (e.g., marriage encounters).

Staple 3: Design living/working space that actually works

Combine family and living rooms for more family living space. Make the kitchen central to the floor plan to place the chef more in the social milieu of the home.

Staple 4: The roles of a leader

Remain open to everyone's concerns and suggestions—don't take others for granted. Discipline consistently and fairly. Reward and encourage openly and frequently.

Staple 5: Measure creatively and meaningfully

Encourage school grades that are high enough to allow entry into university or allow a furthering of careers, whatever they might be. Look for ways to encourage one another to develop each other's self-esteem.

Staple 6: Can the complexity

Limit family members to a maximum of one hour of TV and/ or video games per day per family member. Encourage family games and walks or simple outings.

Staple 7: Inspire others

Watch for opportunities to award a "family member of the moment"—flowers, gifts or simple thanks. Celebrate occasions and events (like someone's getting her or his driver's licence or good grades) with meals or outings.

Behavior: Specific code of behavior (see Staple 5 above)

End Result A:	To attain grades high enough for entry into university.
Measurement:	Keep track of the number of hours spent per day studying for exams and completing daily assignments and projects.
Behavior:	Effective, organized, disciplined study habits.

End Result B:	Higher self-esteem among family members.
Measurement:	Keep track of the number of hugs per day among family members.
Behavior:	Require mandatory hugs after a family member has been absent for half a day or more (i.e., every morning, every evening).

General Code of Behavior:
- to be supportive of one another
- to nurture an atmosphere of love and respect by showing concern and care for each family member
- to create a place of sanctuary where members are loved, not judged; welcomed, not persecuted
- to listen to each other
- to provide constructive encouragement
- to encourage physical touch of a reassuring nature

Bottom Lines:	Visitors come and go easily and happily; family members do the same.

Achievement Challenge 2: Increasing Club Membership

Purpose:	To increase membership so the club's value and influence positively affects more people.
Vision:	To be a club that is responsive to its members and cares about the community.
Focus:	Benefits, value, fun

309

Soft Stuff

Staple 1: Communicating purpose, vision, focus

Visit the purpose, vision and focus of your organization at every meeting. Encourage inspirational meetings with guest speakers or motivational videos.

Staple 2: Training and development

Continually look for better ways to run effective meetings through courses, speakers and experience. Take courses and steadily increase knowledge of how to work effectively with volunteers. Attend one conference a year on how to run voluntary organizations effectively.

Staple 3: Design living/working space that actually works

Treat volunteers like fully paid staff; provide them with office space and equipment to do their tasks. Provide volunteers with ease of access to full-time staff and facilities. Develop their trust.

Staple 4: The roles of a leader

Manage by team membership and not by autocratic leadership or executive committee. Provide high accessibility to leaders. Challenge leadership to treat each member as an important cutomer.

Staple 5: Measure creatively and meaningfully

Develop and distribute a new member's information form that pinpoints reasons for membership. Regularly survey members to determine the club's overall effectiveness. Keep track of the number of suggestion box ideas against the number implemented.

Staple 6: Can the complexity

Institute spending limits below which approval is not required, so that volunteers and staff can get on with the tasks necessary to accomplish purpose, vision and focus. Challenge reasons for committee meetings. Meetings would only take place if the customer for the meeting is defined and determined to be worthwhile. Limit length of committee meetings to 90 minutes.

Staple 7: Inspire others

Regularly acknowledge volunteers, staff and committee members for exceptional service contributions. "Member of the Moment" receives a telephone call from the club president within 24 hours of an achievement and a letter from the club within 72 hours. Openly encourage creativity and innovation during meetings.

Behavior: Specific Code of Behavior

End Result A: To increase membership by 10 percent in the coming year.

Measurement: Monitor the number of face-to-face canvassing visits and follow-ups by volunteers and staff.

Behavior: Canvass all the homes in club's demographic market area–allocate the same number for each committee member.

End Result B: Increase club's overall effectiveness.

Measurement: Regularly compare the number of facility hours available for use with the actual number of hours used.

Behavior: Implement marketing programs that increase awareness of facility availability.

End Result C: To increase membership involvement.

Measurement: Monitor the number of suggestions put forward by members and staff this year versus last year.

Behavior: Implement an action program to implement ideas put forward and a promotion program for communicating those ideas and their source.

General Code of Behavior:
- to be a club that is beneficial to all members
- to ensure substantial value is given for the services offered
- to make sure fun is first and foremost
- to be responsive to the needs of members, staff and volunteers
- to care about everyone associated with the club, its community and its neighborhood

Bottom Lines: A 10-per-cent increase in annual membership.

Although the above examples are general, the more specific your goal, the more focused your footprints should be. I have chosen the examples above because I have no way of knowing which challenges you are facing organizationally. Nevertheless, the above should give you a broad overview of this whole book and the achievement process outlined in it.

You may notice neither example makes any reference to bottom lines except in the bottom line. Although the ultimate objective is important as a starting point, it should not be *the* point. The point, as I've said over and over again in this book, is to concentrate on what must happen above the bottom line to produce that bottom line. Just like a good golf drive, if you focus all your efforts onto what happens before the club makes contact with the ball–the swing–the ball will blast straight down the fairway, right on target.

I hope Alan and I have managed to give you some practical strategies to improve the way you live and work. I welcome your ideas and comments on how we might improve this material for future readers. And, I would appreciate your comments on how this book might have assisted you in your personal and/or professional journey. Write to me c/o Above the Bottom Line, Inc., Box 777, Bragg Creek, Alberta, TOL OKO.

A return to the sea

If your individual or organizational ship is sailing smoothly, count yourself among the fortunate. If your seas are stormy, you are not alone. Regardless of whether the wind is with or against you, there are steps you can take to improve your lot in your personal and organizational life. To take those steps will require risk, commitment and determination. But with a lot of work and a little luck, your journey should not only prove to be personally fruitful, but should also be financially profitable.

If you follow the Footprints in this book in the future, I hope you will be seen as a person people would want to have as a friend, an individual who is a suitable mate or parent, or a leader who is worthy of being followed. On a business level, may the organization in which you work be seen by suppliers as one with which to do business, by its employees as one for which to work and by its customers as one that offers outstanding products, service and value.

May you enjoy your journey, navigate through the woods, step up to those black doors and survive those sinking ships. But most of all, may you have courage.

Ahead of you lies a set of footprints waiting to be made. It could be a trail others will want to follow. You can leave a lasting impression on the world or leave footsteps that vanish with the first rain. The choice is yours.

If you listen, you may hear footsteps...

To reach the port of heaven, we must sail sometimes with the wind and sometimes against it–but we must sail, and not drift, or lie at anchor.

OLIVER WENDELL HOLMES
American physician, author

314

EPILOGUE

He who has a why to live for can bear almost any how.

FRIEDRICH NIETZSCHE
German philosopher

I recently listened to a radio talk show exploring the options available to get people who were on welfare off it. The object, of course, was to get these people off the public purse and to get them to earn their own living. One of the observations brought forward was that many of these "welfare" people did not have the necessary life skills to look after themselves on a day-to-day basis, much less take on a responsible job or have a career.

This challenged me to begin to think whether or not we were missing the point when dealing with some of the problems facing us as human beings. Isn't obtaining the necessary life skills part of training ourselves to have a purpose for our lives, a positive vision of what we want to become and a focus to direct our energies? Wouldn't we be better off helping individuals inside and outside our collective organizations to evolve a purpose, vision and focus? Would such an exercise assist individuals in developing coping strategies for living in our complex and often confusing living and working worlds?

Do we have to wait until we are adults to begin looking at ourselves as functional, dreaming, energized individuals? Are there ways to teach life skills to our children that would positively support them as they journey through life?

Is this skill set learnable? If so, shouldn't we encourage our educational institutions, from elementary schools to universities, to develop courses that instruct students in how to write their purpose, vision and focal points? And shouldn't curriculum should include coaching sessions on how to live positive personal and organizational lives?

What do you think?

What are you going to do about it?

AFTERWORD

As I re-read the material in this book I force myself not to pick up my editing pen. I want to change things, add material, delete some portions. However, I feel like a painter that has completed a painting and knows that making any changes means redoing the entire thing. A minor change in the foreground means massive revision in the background. And I also realize that this kind of fixing and editing could go on forever. So, you've now seen the book, with all of its warts and, I hope, flashes of brilliance. You are the judge. I take sole responsibility for all shortcomings. But, it's time to move on to new material and another painting.

The genesis of this book was from a presentation I developed entitled: **The 18 Characteristics of Successful Organizations and How You Can Achieve Them**. As the book took shape with Alan Hobson, the transition from presentation material to written form was dramatic. This book does not reflect the appearance or texture of what was in my presentation. However, the presentation has been so well received that I have decided to take another run at documenting it in book form. It will be a companion piece to *Above the Bottom Line*. I envision this next business book not as a handbook but rather a commentary on each of the characteristics I see within successful organizations.

We also edited some rather large chunks out of *Above the Bottom Line*. Some were good ideas, they just did not fit this manuscript. I am hoping to incorporate some of this material into the next book. I have also further developed some of the concepts in *Above the Bottom Line* and hope to include some new areas for your consideration–always in the hope that the material will enhance the way you see your professional and personal lives.

317

I would be interested in hearing from you about any material that has impressed you from *Above the Bottom Line,* and would appreciate any ideas or suggestions you might have for future books.

Thank you for sharing this book with me. I hope your journey through it was as challenging, exciting and informative as mine was in writing it.

J. Michael Fuller
Above the Bottom Line Inc.
1993

NOTES

INTRODUCTION

1. Alexander Dru, ed., *The Journals of Kierkegaard 1834-1854*, (Huntington, NY: Fontana Publishing, 1958).

2. Jeremy Main, "Wanted: Leaders Who Can Make a Difference," *Fortune*, September 28, 1987, p. 99.

FOOTPRINT ONE–The Power of Purpose

1. Sam Keen, *Fire in the Belly: On Being a Man* (New York: Bantam Books, 1991), p. 66.

2. David T. Kearns and David A. Nadler, *Prophets in the Dark–How Xerox Reinvented Itself and Beat Back the Japanese* (New York: HarperCollins Publishers, 1992), p. 20.

3. Louis S. Richman, "Struggling to Save Our Kids," *Fortune*, August 10, 1992, pp. 35-36.

4. Peter B. Grazier, *Before It's Too Late* (Pennsylvania: Chadds Ford, Teambuilding, Inc., 1989), p. 5.

5. Art McNeil, *I of the Hurricane* (Toronto: Stoddart, 1987).

6. Anne B. Fisher, "Morale Crisis," *Fortune*, Nov. 18,1991, pp. 70-80.

7. Adapted from *G.E.'s Annual Report*, 1989.

8. Robert Howard, "Values Make the Company, An Interview with Robert Haas," *Harvard Business Review*, Sept.-Oct. 1990, p.135.

9. *Kearns and Nadler*, op. cit., p. 179.

FOOTPRINT TWO–The Value of Vision

1.   David T. Kearns and David A. Nadler, *Prophets in the Dark–How Xerox Reinvented Itself and Beat Back the Japanese* (New York, HarperCollins Publishers, 1992), p. 165.

2.   Adapted from *G.E.'s Annual Report*, 1989.

3.   Robert Howard, "Values Make the Company, An Interview with Robert Haas", *Harvard Business Review*, Sept.-Oct. 1990, pp. 132-144. Purpose statement adapted from Levi Strauss's Aspiration Statement.

FOOTPRINT THREE–The Force of Focus

1.   Peter C. Reid, *Well Made in America, Lessons From Harley-Davidson on Being the Best* (New York, McGraw-Hill, 1992), pp. 161-162.

2.   Ricardo Semler, "Managing Without Managers," *Harvard Business Review*, Sept.-Oct., 1989, p. 77.

3.   Thomas A. Stewart, "A New Way to Wake Up A Giant," *Fortune*, October 22, 1990, p.91.

4.   Brian Dumaine, "Earning More by Moving Faster," *Fortune*, October 7, 1991, p. 94.

FOOTPRINT FOUR–The Soft (Hard-to-Do) Stuff
Part I: Individual

1.   James Allen, *As a Man Thinketh* (World Bible Publishers), pp. 13-14.

FOOTPRINT FOUR–The Soft (Hard-to-Do) Stuff
Part II: Organizational

1. Robert Howard, "Values Make the Company, An Interview with Robert Haas," *Harvard Business Review*, Sept.-Oct. 1990, p.134.

2. Ricardo Semler, "Managing Without Managers," *Harvard Business Review*, Sept.-Oct. 1989, p. 79.

3. Stratford Sherman, "How to Prosper in the Value Decade," *Fortune*, November 30, 1992, p. 103.

4. Al Pipkin, "The controller's role en route to the 21st century," *CMA Magazine*, April 1989, p. 10.

5. David T. Kearns and David A. Nadler, *Prophets in the Dark–How Xerox Reinvented Itself and Beat Back the Japanese* (New York: HarperCollins Publishers, 1992), p. 184.

6. Howard, *"Values Make the Company,"* p. 141.

7. For a more detailed study of why most strategic plans fail, see: "Uses and Misuses of Strategic Planning," Daniel H. Gray, *Harvard Business Review*, Jan.- Feb., 1986, pp. 89-97.

8. Faye Rice, "Champions of Communication," *Fortune*, June 3, 1991, p. 111.

9. *Ibid.*, p. 116.

10. Peter C. Reid, *Well Made in America, Lessons From Harley-Davidson on Being the Best* (New York: McGraw-Hill, 1992), p. 167.

11. Harry B. Bernhard and Cynthia A. Ingols, "Six Lessons From the Corporate Classroom," *Harvard Business Review*, Sept.-Oct. 1988, pp. 40-51.

12. Peter B. Grazier, *Before It's Too Late* (Chadds Ford: Teambuilding, Inc., 1989), p. 105.

13. *Howard*, op. cit., p. 136.

14. Alex Taylor III, "BMW and Mercedes Make Their Move," *Fortune*, Aug. 12, 1991, p. 62.

15. *Inc. Magazine*, December 1991.

16. *Howard*, op. cit., p. 136.

17. *Ibid.*, p. 139.

18. Jan Carlzon, *Moments of Truth* (Cambridge: Ballinger Publishing,1987), p. 88.

19. *Regent College Newsletter.*

20. *Kearns and Nadler*, op. cit., p. 235.

21. *Ibid.*, p. 177.

22. Peter Block, *The Empowered Manager* (San Francisco: Jossey-Bass Inc., 1987), p. xiv.

23. For more on coping with the system, see Lawrence M. Miller's *Barbarians to Bureaucrats–Corporate Life Cycle Strategies,* Ballantine Books, 1989.

24. James M. Kouzes and Barry Z. Posner, "The Credibility Factor: What Followers Expect From Their Leaders," *Management Review*, January 1990, pp. 29-33.

25. Max DePree, *Leadership Is an Art* (New York: Doubleday, 1989), p. 15.

26. Dr. D. Chris Anderson and Craig J. Nichols, "A Technology of Lasting Change in Employee Performance: A Primer to Organizational Behavior Management (OBM)," working paper, no date reported.

27. *Reid*, op. cit., p. 178.

28. Carl Sewell and Paul B. Brown, *Customers for Life* (New York: Simon & Schuster, 1990), pp. 83-84.

29. *Ibid.*, p. 91.

30. For more on measuring for results, see "Successful Change Programs Begin with Results," Robert H. Schaffer and Harvey A. Thomson, *Harvard Business Review*, Jan.-Feb. 1992.

FOOTPRINT FIVE–Brilliancies in Behavior
Part I: Individual

1. Jeffrey D. Imbach, *The Recovery of Love* (New York: The Crossroad Publishing Company, 1992), p. 94.

2. W. Timothy Gallwey, *The Inner Game of Golf* (New York: Random House, 1981), p. 95.

3. Alan Weiss, *Managing for Peak Performance: A Guide to the Power (and Pitfalls) of Personal Style* (Harper Collins, 1990). See also David W. Johnson, *Reaching Out: Interpersonal Effectiveness and Self-Actualization*, (4th Edition, Prentice-Hall, 1990).

FOOTPRINT FIVE–Brilliancies inBehavior
Part II: Organizational

1. For more on this see: "Champions of Communication," *Fortune*, June 3, 1991.

2. Bo Burlingham and Curtis Hartman, "Cowboy Capitalist," *Inc. Magazine*, January 1989, p. 66.

3. Strategic planning document, Crestar Energy, 1992

4. *General Electric, Annual Report*, 1989. Also, for more on GE and how they bring their purpose, vision and focus alive see, "GE Keeps Those Ideas Coming," *Fortune*, August 19, 1991.

5. *Inside Guide*, December 1991.

6. Canadian Hunter company handout and employee handbook

7. David T. Kearns and David A. Nadler, *Prophets in the Dark–How Xerox Reinvented Itself and Beat Back the Japanese* (New York: HarperCollins Publishers, 1992), p. 208.

8. *Ibid.*, p. 159.

9. *The Forum Corporation, consumer survey results*, Boston, MA, USA. I0. Jan Carlzon, "Leadership Is Like a Blueprint for a Cathedral," remarks by Jan Carlzon to the Marketing Society, London, England, November 1985.

FOOTPRINT SIX – The Bottom Line
Part I: Individual

1. Richard Harrison, "Strategies for a New Age," *Human Resource Management*, Fall 1983. Vol. 22, No. 3, pp. 211 and 213.

2. Letter to the editor, *Fortune,* December 28, 1992.

FOOTPRINT SIX–The Bottom Line
Part II: Organizational

1. Ralph Stayer, "How I Learned to Let My Workers Lead," *Harvard Business Review*, November-December, 1990, pp. 66-83.

2. Approval for inclusion in this book was received by telephone, December 24, 1992, from Mr. Ralph Stayer. Johnsonville's evaluation has since changed and the new method/form will be included in his own soon-to-be published book, *Flight of the Buffalo.*